Making Out in Turkish

Making Out in Turkish

Ashley Carman

TUTTLE PUBLISHING
Tokyo • Rutland, Vermont • Singapore

Published by Tuttle Publishing, an imprint of Periplus Editions (HK) Ltd., with editorial offices at 364 Innovation Drive, North Clarendon, Vermont 05759 U.S.A. and at 61 Tai Seng Avenue #02-12, Singapore 534167.

Library of Congress Cataloging-in-Publication Data
Carman, Ashley.
Making Out in Turkish / Ashley Carman. —1st ed.
p. cm.
ISBN 978-0-8048-4025-5 (pbk.)
1. Turkish language—Conversation and phrase books—English. I. Title.
PL127.C37 2009
494'.3583421—dc22
2008042074

ISBN 978-0-8048-4025-5

Distributed by

North America, Latin America & Europe
Tuttle Publishing
364 Innovation Drive
North Clarendon, VT 05759-9436 U.S.A.
Tel: 1 (802) 773-8930
Fax: 1 (802) 773-6993
info@tuttlepublishing.com
www.tuttlepublishing.com

Asia-Pacific
Berkeley Books Pte. Ltd.
61 Tai Seng Avenue #02-12
Singapore 534167
Tel: (65) 6280-1330
Fax: (65) 6280-6290
inquiries@periplus.com.sg
www.periplus.com

First edition
12 11 10 09 10 9 8 7 6 5 4 3 2 1

Printed in Singapore

I dedicate this book to my only rose without thorns, my mom whose infinite love surrounds all that I do. I thank you wholeheartedly for always keeping me near and dear to your heart even though I have been far from your eyes. I love you more than yesterday, less than tomorrow.

Bu kitabı, beni her zaman koşulsuz bağrına basan, hudutsuz sevgisiyle uzakları aşıp yanıbaşımda olan dikensiz tek gülüme, canım anneciğime armağan ediyorum. Gözden ıraktayken bile beni hep gönlüne yakın tutan tek kişi olduğun ve değeri kelimelere sığmayan tüm fedakarlıkların için teşekkür ederim. Seni çok seviyorum. İyi ki varsın.

Contents

Introduction 9

1. What's Up? 25
2. Basic Phrases 36
3. Got a Minute? 42
4. Hey There! 50
5. Look at That 55
6. Coming & Going 58
7. Eat, Drink & Be Merry 63
8. I Like It! 73
9. Fighting & Curses 79
10. Going Out 85
11. On the Phone 94
12. Getting Serious 99
13. Lovers' Language 102
14. Trouble in Paradise 111

Expressions & Proverbs 118

Introduction

Do you have an interest in learning Turkish, but are discouraged by the idea of memorizing your way through hard-to-follow lessons? *Making Out in Turkish* is for you. This book is your ticket to learning Turkish like you learned your mother tongue: naturally. With this engaging, fun and practical guide, you will be able to express yourself in everyday informal dialogue in no time.

Making Out in Turkish is modular in that every chapter is independent so you can read through chapters in whichever order fits your specific dialogue needs.

Whether you are trying to make friends, communicate with a lover or travel abroad, this is your passport to making out in Turkish.

TURKEY AT A GLANCE

Türkiye Cumhuriyeti (the Republic of Turkey) is the official name of the country. It's also known as **Türkiye**.

Location

Turkey is situated at the intersection of two continents, Asia and Europe.

It is surrounded by the Mediterranean, the Aegean, the Marmara and the Black Sea. It has an area of approximately 800,000 square km and a total coastline of 8,333 km. It has borders with Georgia and Armenia to the northeast, Iran and Iraq to the southeast, Bulgaria and Greece to the northwest and Syria to the south.

Capital

Ankara is the capital of the Republic of Turkey.

Many people mistakenly think İstanbul is the capital city of Turkey. It's the largest city of Turkey, but not the capital. During a 2,000-year period, İstanbul (historically, Constantinople) was the capital city of four successive empires. It was the capital of the Roman Empire during 330–395, of the Byzantine Empire during 395–1204 and again during 1261–1453, of the Latin empire during 1204–1261 and of the Ottoman Empire during 1453–1922.

Flag

The Turkish flag depicts a centered white crescent-moon with a star inside, on a red field.

National Anthem

The *İstiklâl Marşı* ("Independence March") is the national anthem of Turkey, adopted on March 12, 1921. When a nationwide competition was organized to select a suitable national anthem, 724 poems were submitted. The Turkish Grand National Assembly unanimously chose a 10-verse poem written by famous poet Mehmet Akif Ersoy.

Religion

Islam is the religion of the majority of Turkish people (99.8%). Minority religions include Christianity and Judaism. Turkey is not governed by Islamic law.

Atatürk

Mustafa Kemal Atatürk is the name of the founder of the Republic of Turkey. *Atatürk* means "the father of the Turks." Despite his limited resources, he worked towards transforming the Ottoman Empire into a modern country. Some of his important reforms are:

- Change from the Arabic alphabet to Latin alphabet
- Foundation of a secular state (religion and state were separated)
- Introduction of monogamy
- Change from the Islamic calendar to the Gregorian calendar
- Women were given the right to vote and to be elected
- Modern dress code

The Republic of Turkey was established on October 29, 1923. Atatürk was the first president. He is a national hero to the Turkish people and his quotes, pictures, and monuments can be found everywhere in Turkey, from inside business offices to out on the streets.

TURKEY'S CULTURE

Turkey has a very diverse culture combining elements belonging to the Ottoman Empire, Europe and Islam. While living modern lives, the Turkish people make efforts to maintain their traditions.

You'll see that the culture of Turkey varies depending on the region and the ethnic background of its inhabitants. In big cities, the culture is very similar to Europe's. The culture in rural parts of Turkey is more traditional.

Greetings

- When meeting someone, it's customary to shake hands.
- Close friends and family members normally greet each other by kissing on one or both cheeks.
- Turkish people demonstrate respect for the elderly by kissing their elder's right hand then placing their own forehead against the elder's hand. When you enter a

room, it's customary to greet the most elderly person first.

- Turks do not require as much personal space as some other cultures, and will stand close to you while conversing. Too much distance between people, for them, implies not being friendly and sincere.
- It's vital that you maintain eye contact while speaking since Turks take this as a sign of sincerity.
- During business meetings, it is considered rude to get to the point too abruptly. Turks will first inquire about your family and so on to establish trust, and will expect the same from you.

Cuisine

- Mealtime is an occasion for getting together with family and friends to engage in good conversation. **"Yemek içmek bahane, amaç muhabbet"** is a common saying in Turkey. It means "To eat and to drink is an excuse, the goal is to have a good conversation."
- It's not polite to eat in front of someone without offering to share. Turks will offer to share their snack with you, or even the food on their plate. It's polite to take some if you want them to continue to eat with comfort. Otherwise they will not feel at ease eating in front of you. There is a Turkish idiom reflecting the importance of this gesture: "One eats while another does not, this is why the Judgement Day arrives." If you are the one with food or snack, offer to share to demonstrate your own hospitality.
- Although on special occasions they do go to restaurants, Turkish people mostly eat home-cooked meals.
- Bread is served and eaten at every meal in Turkey.
- A typical Turkish breakfast, usually light, consists of tea, feta cheese, bread, butter, eggs, marmalade or honey,

and olives. Dinner is the main meal of the day and may consist of several courses.

- People drink Turkish tea at almost every breakfast. Turkish tea is served in a glass accompanied by a small spoon to stir sugar with, and a saucer that holds the glass. The tea is prepared without sugar and generally one or two cubes of sugar will be placed on the saucer. Otherwise, a bowl of granulated sugar will accompany the tea. Turkish people do not drink "a glass" of tea. Glasses are refilled constantly unless you specify otherwise. It's a general practice to leave your teaspoon across the top of your tea glass to indicate that you do not want any more tea. Also, it's polite to say to the host "**Ziyade olsun**," meaning "May you enjoy abundance," when you've finished drinking your tea.
- Turkish coffee is traditionally prepared black (without sugar). It can, however, be sweetened according to taste; you should make sure to specify when you order if you want it sweetened. The bitter coffee grounds at the bottom of the cup are not meant to be drunk.
- When eating in a restaurant, the host pays for the meal. The concept of dividing the bill is foreign to Turkish people. It's polite to offer to pay, but you would not be allowed to do so by the host. The best thing to do is to graciously thank your host. At a later occasion, you can invite them for dinner at a restaurant of your choice, this time with you being the host.
- The national drink is **rakı**, an aniseed-flavored clear grape brandy, similar to Greek ouzo or French pastis. It's served mixed with water.
- You should always compliment the cook who prepared the meal by saying "**Eline sağlık**," which means "Bless your hands."

Visiting

- Turkish people maintain close-knit relationships with immediate families, relatives, friends and neighbors. They phone and visit each other often.
- Most houses are floored with handmade Turkish carpets. Generally, people will remove their shoes at their door and replace them with house slippers. Hosts expect that their guests will do the same.
- Visitors are always offered something to drink, such as tea or coffee served with dessert or Turkish pastries. Even if you have a full stomach, it is impolite to decline.

Other Facts about Turkey

- Turkey is the only secular Muslim country among the Muslim countries in the world.
- İstanbul is the only city in the world that's built on two continents: Europe and Asia.
- Turkish culture has a strong belief about the "evil eye." It's thought that even well-intentioned compliments include a conscious or unconscious dose of envy. To protect against the evil eye, the Turkish people use a dark blue bead that has a turquoise eye shape in the middle. Some of the places you'll most commonly see the usage of evil eye beads, called **nazar boncuğu**, are on baby clothes, at the entrances of houses and offices and even as jewelry.
- When a loved one leaves for a journey, it is customary to pour a bucket of water behind the car or taxi he or she takes, in the hopes that the journey will be smooth and the loved one will reach the destination safely.
- The Trojan Wars took place in western Turkey, and a replica of the Trojan horse rests today in Çanakkale.
- St. Nicholas, also known as Santa Claus, was born in Demre in Turkey.

- Perhaps for some foreigners, the symbol of Turkey is the red Ottoman Empire fez; yet, it's illegal to wear a fez in Turkey. After the establishment of the Republic of Turkey in 1923, Atatürk, the founder of the country, enforced the modern dress code, banning fez.
- Dolmabahçe Palace in İstanbul has the world's largest chandelier, weighing approximately 4.5 tons.
- The character Aslan's name in C. S. Lewis' well known book series the Chronicles of Narnia actually means "lion" in Turkish.
- Turkish delight, **lokum**, pronounced *loh-koom*, is a confection made from starch and sugar. It has a soft, jelly-like and sometimes sticky consistency, and is often packaged and eaten in small cubes that are dusted with powdered sugar. Besides the plain Turkish delight, there are various types flavored with rose water, pistachio, walnut, lemon, hazelnuts, and more.
- Sabiha Gökçen, the adopted daughter of the founder of Turkey, Atatürk, was the world's first female combat pilot.

THE LANGUAGE

Turkish is the official language of Turkey, spoken by 90% of the population. Minority languages are Kurdish, Greek, Armenian and Hebrew.

Turkish is a very ancient language dating back 5,500 to 8,500 years. It uses a modified Latin alphabet which has a phonetic structure. The alphabet consists of 29 letters, 8 of which are vowels.

Each letter has one sound associated with it and it sounds the same all the time. In English the "a" in dad and the "a" in darling sound different, yet in Turkish, you will not encounter variations in the pronunciation of a letter.

Also to keep in mind: Turkish does not use diphthongs (two or more letters combined to make a new sound).

Vowel diphthongs such as **ea** (gr**ea**t) or consonant diphthongs such as **th** (**th**ere) do not exist in Turkish. The Turkish name Mithat is pronounced as Miht–**h**aht, sounding both the **t** and the **h** letters (*not* Mih-**th**aht pronouncing **th** as one sound).

Vowels

Turkish Letter	Transcription	Sounds Like	Example	Meaning
a	*a*	art	**araba**	car
e	*e*	egg	**ev**	house
ı	*ə*	curtain	**ışık**	light
	The letter **ı** doesn't have an English equivalent but you can hear the sound in words such as lab**e**l, ov**e**n, penc**i**l, farm**e**r, op**e**n. If you pronounce the word "higher" as you would in English, you would also be saying "no" (**hayır**) in Turkish.			
i	*ih*	if	**iyi**	good
o	*oh*	open	**okul**	school
ö	*ö*	urge	**öğrenci**	student
	The letter **ö** doesn't have an English equivalent but you can hear the sound in words such as b**ir**d, c**ur**se, g**ir**l, h**er**, t**ur**n, f**ur**, s**ir**. If you pronounce the word "dirt" as you would in English, you would also be saying "four" (**dört**) in Turkish.			

u	*oo*	pull	**uçak**	airplane

The sound of the letter **u** can be heard in English words such as pull, push, put.

ü	*ü*	dew	**üzüm**	grape

The letter **ü** doesn't have an exact English equivalent; try slowly saying the exclamation "ewwww!", like someone might react to a disliked food, in order to get a sense of this letter's sound. You can hear a similar sound in words such as dew, stew, and few.

Consonants

Turkish Letter	Transcription	Sounds Like	Example	Meaning
b	*b*	boy	**baba**	father
c	*j*	jam	**cevap**	answer
ç	*ch*	chance	**çay**	tea
d	*d*	dog	**defter**	notebook
f	*f*	fine	**fincan**	cup
g	*g*	get	**gece**	night
ğ	*gh*			

It is hard to explain the pronunciation of **ğ** since English does not have a similar sound. It sounds like the *r* in French as in "merci" (thank you). Think of the sound you make when you gargle. If you find it's too hard to sound it, just ignore it, lengthening the letter before it; for example, **öğrenci** (student) would be pronounced as *öö-rehn-jih*. In this book, we'll transcribe this letter as *gh*.

h	*h*	hello	**haber**	news
j	*zh*	treasure	**jilet**	razor
k	*k*	keep	**kitap**	book
l	*l*	lime	**lütfen**	please
m	*m*	map	**merhaba**	hello
n	*n*	nice	**numara**	number
p	*p*	puppy	**para**	money
r	*r*	rest	**renk**	color
s	*s*	soda	**su**	water
ş	*sh*	ship	**şey**	thing
t	*t*	tip	**tatlı**	sweet
v	*v*	very	**ve**	and
y	*y*	yes	**yol**	road
z	*z*	zero	**zaman**	time

Double Letters

In Turkish there are no silent letters. When you encounter double letters, remember to pronounce both. For example **saat** (clock) is pronounced as *sah-aht*, not *saht*.

The vowel harmony rule and agglutination are the backbones of the Turkish language.

Vowel Harmony Rule

This rule requires that vowels in the first syllable of a word should be harmonious with the subsequent syllables. If the first syllable has soft vowels (**e, i, ü, ö**) then the following syllable should also have soft vowels. If the first syllable has hard vowels (**a, ı, u, o**) then the following syllable should have hard vowels.

erkek (man) **kadın** (woman) **sevgi** (love)

Foreign words adopted by Turkish do not follow this rule.

aktör (actor) **taksi** (taxi) **televizyon** (television)

Agglutination

Turkish is an agglutination language and suffixes are added to the words, constructing extended words.

Let's take the English word "nation" for example. By adding a particular ending, it is possible to agglutinate (extend) it to become "national," "nationality" or "nationally." Similarly, Turkish uses suffixes that change the meanings and even grammatical functions of words. Nouns, adjectives, pronouns, tenses, even words like "from," "at," "in" are suffixed following the vowel harmony rule. For example:

ev	a house	**arkadaş**	a friend
evim	my house	**arkadaşım**	my friend
evler	houses	**arkadaşlar**	friends
evde	at the house	**arkadaşta**	at a friend
evden	from the house	**arkadaştan**	from my friend

Nouns

Turkish does not use articles such as the English words "the," "a" or "an." However, **bir** (one) can be used before a noun to represent the indefinite articles "a" or "an."

kitap	book	**defter**	notebook
bir kitap	a book	**bir defter**	a notebook

To make a noun plural, add **-ler** or **-lar** following the harmony rule. Adjectives always come before their nouns and they do not agree in number.

kitaplar	books	**defterler**	notebooks
beş kitap	five books	**beş defter**	five notebooks

If **bir** is used, adjectives come before **bir**.

büyük kitap	big book
büyük bir kitap	a big book

küçük defter	small notebook
küçük bir defter	a small notebook

Questions

Question sentences are formed by adding a question word at the beginning of a sentence. See Chapter 2 for some useful question words.

Another way to form a question sentence is by adding the **-mi** suffix in accordance with the harmony rule. Do not confuse the **-mi** question suffix with the **-mi** negation word (explained below). Notice that the question suffix is always written separate from the word it's added to:

Adınız Can mı?
Is your name Can?

İçecek bir şey ister misin?
Do you want something to drink?

Türk müsün?
Are you Turkish?

You can also add question tags such as "right?" or "okay?" to a sentence:

Bu akşam seni arayacağım, tamam mı?
I will call you tonight, okay?

Bu hafta sonu diskoya gidiyoruz, değil mi?
We will go to the disco this weekend, right?

Negation

To make a *noun* or *adjective* negative, simply add **değil** at the end of it. This could roughly be translated as "not" in English.

önemli
important

önemli değil
not important

arabam beyaz
my car is white

arabam beyaz değil
my car is not white

To make a *verb* negative, add the **-mi** suffix at the root of the verb with accordance to the harmony rule. It could roughly be translated as "don't" in English.

Gitmek istiyorum
I want to go

Gitmek istemiyorum
I don't want to go

Seni anlıyorum
I understand you

Seni anlamıyorum
I don't understand you

What's Up? 1

Have a nice day.	**İyi günler.** *ih-YİH gün-LEHR*
Good morning.	**Günaydın.** *gü-nahy-DƏN*
Good night.	**İyi geceler.** *ih-YİH geh-jeh-LEHR*
Hello.	**Merhaba.** *mehr-hah-BAH*
How are you?	**Nasılsın?** *nah-səl-SƏN?*
I'm fine, and you?	**İyiyim, ya sen?** *ih-yih-YİHM, yah sehn?*

What's your name?	**İsmin ne?** *ihs-MİHN neh?*
My name is Can.	**İsmim Can.** *ihs-MİHN jahn*
Nice meeting you.	**Memnun oldum.** *mehm-NOON ohl-DOOM*
Nice meeting you too.	**Ben de memnun oldum.** *behn deh mehm-NOON ohl-DOOM*
Are you Turkish?	**Türk müsün?** *türk mü-sün?*
Do you speak English?	**İngilizce biliyor musun?** *ihn-gih-lihz-JEH bih-lih-YOHR moo-soon?*
My Turkish is not very good.	**Türkçem pek iyi değil.** *türk-CHEHM pehk ih-YİH deh-GHİHL*
Can you repeat?	**Tekrar eder misin?** *tehk-RAHR eh-DEHR mih-sihn?*
What are you doing?	**Ne yapıyorsun?** *neh yah-pə-yohr-SOON?*
Where are you?	**Nerdesin?** *nehr-deh-SİHN?*
Where are you from?	**Nerelisin?** *neh-reh-lih-SİHN?*

Where are you going?	**Nereye gidiyorsun?** *neh-reh-YEH gih-dih-yohr-SOON?*
What's with you?	**Neyin var senin?** *neh-YİHN vahr seh-NİHN?*
Why are you sad?	**Neden üzgünsün?** *neh-DEHN üz-gün-SÜN?*
Don't be sad!	**Üzülme!** *ü-zül-MEH!*
How are you feeling?	**Kendini nasıl hissediyorsun?** *kehn-dih-NİH nah-SƏL hihs-seh-dih-yohr-SOON?*
I'm happy.	**Mutluyum.** *moot-loo-YOOM*
I'm tired.	**Yorgunum.** *yohr-goo-NOOM*
I'm scared.	**Korkuyorum.** *kohr-koo-yoh-ROOM*
I'm not feeling well.	**Kendimi iyi hissetmiyorum.** *kehn-dih-MİH ih-YİH hihs-seht-mih-yoh-ROOM*
How is Can?	**Can nasıl?** *jahn nah-SƏL?*
Can I ask you a question?	**Sana bir soru sorabilir miyim?** *sah-NAH bihr soh-ROO soh-rah-bih-LİHR mih-yihm?*

Can you do me a favor?	**Bana bir iyilik yapar mısın?** *bah-NAH bihr ih-yih-LİHK yah-PAHR mə-sən?*
Can you help me?	**Bana yardım eder misin?** *bah-NAH yahr-DƏM eh-DEHR mih-sihn?*
How can I help you? (formal)	**Size nasıl yardımcı olabilirim?** *sih-ZEH nah-SƏL yahr-dəm-JƏ oh-lah-bih-lih-RİHM?*
How can I help you? (informal)	**Sana nasıl yardımcı olabilirim?** *sah-NAH nah-SƏL yahr-dəm-JƏ oh-lah-bih-lih-RİHM?*
Maybe.	**Belki.** *behl-KİH*
Nothing.	**Hiç birşey** *hihch bihr-SHEHY*
I don't think so.	**Öyle zannetmiyorum.** *öy-LEH zahn-neht-mih-yoh-ROOM*
I think so.	**Öyle zannediyorum** *öy-LEH zahn-neh-dih-yoh-ROOM*
I am busy.	**Meşgulüm** *Mehsh-goo-LÜM*
Can I come in?	**Girebilir miyim?** *gih-reh-bih-LİHR mih-yihm?*

Come in!	**Gir!** *gihr!*
Come here!	**Buraya gel!** *boo-rah-YAH gehl!*
Not yet.	**Henüz değil.** *heh-NÜZ deh-GHİHL*
Gladly / with pleasure.	**Memnuniyetle.** *mehm-NOO-nih-yeht-leh*
I'm sure.	**Eminim.** *eh-mih-NİHM*
I'm not sure.	**Emin değilim.** *eh-MİHN deh-ghih-LİHM*
Congratulations.	**Tebrikler.** *tehb-rihk-LEHR*
I congratulate you.	**Tebrik ederim.** *tehb-RİHK eh-deh-RİHM*
Good luck.	**İyi şanslar.** *ih-YİH shahns-LAHR*
I'm happy for you.	**Senin adına sevindim.** *seh-NİHN ah-də-NAH seh-vihn-DİHM*
Are you serious?	**Ciddi misin?** *jihd-DİH mih-sihn?*

You're lying.	**Yalan söylüyorsun.** *yah-LAHN söy-lü-yohr-SOON*
I'm serious.	**Ciddiyim.** *jihd-dih-YİHM*
It can't be!	**Olamaz!** *oh-lah-MAHZ!*
I don't believe you.	**İnanmıyorum.** *ih-nahn-mə-yoh-ROOM*
I can't believe that.	**İnanamıyorum.** *ih-nah-nah-mə-yoh-ROOM*
Really?	**Sahi mi?** *sah-HİH mih?*

You can also say **hadi ya** or **yapma ya** as expressions of disbelief. These colloquial expressions can be translated as "you don't say!"

You're joking, right?	**Şaka yapıyorsun, değil mi?** *shah-KAH yah-pə-yohr-SOON, deh-GHİHL mih?*

Turkish natives say **di mi** instead of **değil mi**. It's not proper language but colloquial.

I'm kidding.	**Şaka yapıyorum.** *shah-KAH yah-pə-yoh-ROOM*

You could also say "**Şaka şaka**" in a joking manner.

I'm not kidding.	**Şaka yapmıyorum.** *shah-KAH yahp-mə-yoh-ROOM*

I don't know.	**Bilmiyorum.** *bihl-mih-yoh-ROOM*
I hope so.	**Öyle umarım.** *öy-LEH oo-mah-RƏM*
I suppose so.	**Galiba.** *gah-lih-BAH*
Cool!	**Harika!** *hah-rih-KAH!*
Me too.	**Ben de.** *behn deh*

This is also used to mean "me neither." So if someone says "I'm not hungry" (**Aç değilim**) and you want to say "Me neither," you would say "**Ben de.**"

Enough already!	**Yeter artık!** *yeh-TEHR ahr-TƏK!*
Don't talk nonsense!	**Saçmalama!** *SACH-mah-lah-mah!*
It's important.	**Önemli.** *ö-nehm-LİH*

It's not important.	**Önemli değil.** *ö-nehm-LİH deh-GHİHL*
It doesn't concern me.	**Beni ilgilendirmez.** *beh-NİH ihl-gih-lehn-dihr-MEHZ*
Never mind.	**Boşver.** *bohsh-VEHR*
Don't be stupid!	**Aptal olma!** *ahp-TAHL ohl-MAH!*
Don't talk like an idiot!	**Aptal aptal konuşma!** *ahp-TAHL ahp-TAHL koh-noosh-MAH!*
Are you crazy or what?!	**Deli misin ne?!** *deh-LİH mih-sihn neh?!*
I don't mind.	**Benim için bir mahsuru yok.** *beh-NİHM ih-CHİHN bihr mahh-soo-ROO yohk*
There is no problem.	**Sorun yok.** *soh-ROON yohk*
It's not necessary.	**Gerek yok.** *geh-REHK yohk*
Go away!	**Defol!** *deh-FOHL!*
Get out of here!	**Defol buradan!** *deh-FOHL boo-rah-DAHN!*

Why not? **Neden olmasın?**
neh-DEHN ohl-mah-SƏN?

I have an idea. **Bir fikrim var.**
bihr fihk-RİHM vahr

Count on me. **Bana güven.**
bah-NAH gü-VEHN

Excuse me! **Afedersin!**
ah-feh-dehr-SİHN!

This is used to get someone's attention or to interrupt a conversation.

Excuse me. **Pardon.**
pahr-DOHN

Use this if you accidentally bump into someone, or if you need to get by.

I apologize. **Özür dilerim.**
ö-ZÜR dih-leh-RİHM

What's it to you? **Sana ne?**
sah-NAH neh?

Mind your own business!	**Sen kendi işine bak!** *sehn kehn-DİH ih-shih-NEH bahk!*
Calm down.	**Sakin ol.** *sah-KİHN ohl*
Sit down!	**Otur!** *oh-TOOR!*
Shut up!	**Kapa çeneni!** *kah-PAH che-neh-NİH!*
Can you be quiet, please.	**Susar mısın, lütfen.** *soo-SAHR mə-sən lüt-FEHN*
Come on!	**Hadi!** *hah-DEE!*

This is an expression widely used in everyday conversations. **Hadi** may be used several ways depending on the situation. **Hadi gidelim** means "let's go." **Hadi ya!** is used to express shock. **E hadi!** is used to express impatience when you expect someone to do something and they are slow about it. At the end of a phone conversation, **Tamam hadi** means "Okay, that's all for now."

Don't worry.	**Endişelenme.** *ehn-dih-sheh-lehn-MEH*
I have to go.	**Gitmeliyim.** *giht-meh-lih-YİHM*
I don't need your opinion.	**Senin görüşüne ihtiyacım yok.** *seh-NİHN gö-rü-shü-NEH ihh-tih-yah-JƏM yohk*

My mind is somewhere else.	**Aklım başka bir yerde.** *ahk-LƏM bahsh-KAH bihr yehr-DEH*
See you later.	**Sonra görüşürüz.** *sohn-RAH gö-rü-shü-RÜZ*

Bye.	**Hoşçakal.** *hohsh-chah-KAHL*

This is used *by* the person leaving.

Bye.	**Güle güle.** *gü-LEH gü-LEH*

This is used *to* the person leaving.

Basic Phrases 2

Mrs. **Bayan / Hanım**
bah-YAHN / hahn-İM

Note that **bayan** is used before the last name and **hanım** is used after the first name. Jane Smith would be addressed as either "**bayan Smith**" or "**Jane hanəm.**" Both are correct, and are used interchangeably. You can use this for both married and unmarried women.

Mr. **Bay / Bey**
bahy / behy

Bay is used before the last name and **bey** is used after the first name. John Smith would be addressed as either "**bay Smith**" or "**John bey**." Here also, both are correct, and are used interchangeably.

Ma'am **Hanfendi**
hahn-fehn-DİH

You would use this when addressing a woman without using her name or last name.

Sir **Beyefendi**
behy-eh-fehn-DİH

You would use this when addressing a man without using his name or last name.

Yes **Evet**
e-VEHT

No	**Hayır** *hah-YƏR*
Okay	**Tamam** *ta-MAHM*
But…	**Ama…** *ah-MAH…*
Because.	**Çünkü.** *chün-KÜ*
What?	**Ne?** *neh?*
Who?	**Kim?** *kihm?*
Whose?	**Kimin?** *kih-MİHN?*
Where?	**Nerede?** *neh-reh-DEH?*
To where?	**Nereye?** *neh-reh-YEH?*

From where? **Nereden?**
neh-reh-DEHN?

When? **Ne zaman?**
neh zah-MAHN?

Why? **Neden / Niçin / Niye?**
neh-DEHN / nih-CHİHN / nih-YEH?

There is no difference among these three options; they can be used interchangeably.

How? **Nasıl?**
nah-SƏL?

This **Bu**
boo

That **Şu**
shoo

Maybe **Belki**
behl-KİH

I **Ben**
behn

You **Sen**
sehn

He / she / it **O**
oh

We **Biz**
bihz

You (plural) **Sizler**
sihz-LEHR

They **Onlar**
ohn-LAHR

Please **Lütfen**
lüt-FEHN

Thank you **Teşekkür ederim / Sağol / Teşekkürler.**
teh-shehk-KÜR eh-deh-RİHM / sah-GHOHL / teh-shehk-kür-LEHR

These options all convey the same meaning and are used interchangeably. If you are having difficulty with pronouncing the **ğ** letter in **Sağol** above, you can omit it and say "*sah-ohl.*" You will still be understood.

You're welcome. **Rica ederim.**
rih-jah eh-deh-RİHM

What's it to me? **Bana ne?**
bah-NAH neh?

This is used to mean "I don't care."

What is it to you? **Sana ne?**
sah-NAH neh?

This is used to imply "it doesn't concern you."

I'm only looking. **Sadece bakıyorum.**
sah-deh-JEH bah-kə-yoh-ROOM

It's common, especially in open markets, for sellers to be assertive. You might often hear sellers yell "**Abi buyur**" which means "Brother, come on in." Don't feel pressured. If you are not interested, it's okay to keep walking.

Welcome. **Hoşgeldin.**
hohsh-gehl-DİHN

This is a greeting by the host.

I am happy to be here. **Hoş bulduk.**
hohsh bool-DOOK

This is the customary response by the visitor.

Would you like something to drink? **İçecek bir şey alır mısın?**
ih-cheh-JEHK bihr-shehy ah-LƏR mə-sən?

A glass of tea, please. **Bir bardak çay, lütfen.**
bihr bahr-DAHK chahy, lüt-FEHN

If you ask for "tea" in Turkey, a glass of hot Turkish tea is what will be understood. Iced tea is not common in Turkey but if you mention that you would like your tea with ice and in a larger cup than a tea glass, it would be accommodated.

How much is this? **Bu ne kadar?**
boo neh kah-DAHR?

That's too expensive. **Çok pahalı.**
chohk pah-hah-LƏ

I'm not buying that with this price. **Bu fiyatla almam.**
boo fih-yaht-LAH ahl-MAHM

If we agree on the price, I would buy it. **Fiyatta anlaşırsak alırım.**
fih-yaht-TAH ahn-lah-shər-SAHK ah-lə-RƏM

If you sell it for a cheaper price, I would buy it. **Biraz ucuza verirsen alırım.**
bih-RAHZ oo-joo-ZAH veh-rihr-SEHN ah-lə-RƏM

What's your final price? **Son fiyatın ne?**
sohn fih-yah-TƏN neh?

It's normal to bargain in Turkey. It's okay to offer a bargain price based on the selling price. Often, the buyer and seller agree and shake hands to close the deal.

All right, we agree. **Peki anlaştık.**
peh-KEE, ahn-lahsh-TƏK

Okay, I'm buying it. **Tamam, alıyorum.**
tah-MAHM ah-lə-yoh-ROOM

Thank you for the tea. **Çay için teşekkürler.**
chahy ih-CHİHN teh-shehk-kür-LEHR

If you're in a shop, you might encounter sellers who offer you something to drink, commonly a glass of hot Turkish tea. It's part of Turkish hospitality and not a sales ploy.

Have a good day. **İyi günler.**
ih-YİH gün-LEHR

Got a Minute? 3

One moment, please.	**Bir dakika, lütfen / Bir saniye, lütfen.** *bihr dah-kih-KAH, lüt-FEHN / bihr sah-nih-YEH, lüt-FEHN*

Literally **bir dakika** means "one minute." You can also use **bir saniye** which means "one second." Just as in English, both are used interchangeably to mean the more general "one moment."

When?	**Ne zaman?** *neh zah-MAHN?*
Till when?	**Ne zamana kadar?** *neh zah-mah-NAH kah-DAHR?*
At what time?	**Saat kaçta?** *sah-AHT kahch-TAH?*
Is that too early?	**Çok mu erken?** *chohk moo ehr-KEHN?*
Is that too late?	**Çok mu geç?** *chohk moo gehch?*
When is convenient for you?	**Ne zaman sana uygun?** *neh zah-MAHN sah-NAH ooy-GOON?*

What day is it convenient for you?	**Hangi gün sana uygun?** *hahn-GİH gün sah-NAH ooy-GOON?*
Today	**Bugün** *boo-GÜN*
Yesterday	**Dün** *dün*
Tomorrow	**Yarın** *yah-RƏN*
The day before yesterday	**Dünden evvelki gün** *dün-DEHN ehv-vehl-KİH gün*
How about tomorrow?	**Yarına ne dersin?** *yah-rə-NAH neh dehr-SİHN?*
How about (day)?	**(...) gününe ne dersin?** *(...) gü-nü-NEH neh dehr-SİHN?*
How about Monday?	**Pazartesi gününe ne dersin?** *pah-zahr-teh-SİH gü-nü-NEH neh dehr-SİHN?*

Tuesday / Wednesday / Thursday	**Salı / Çarşamba / Perşembe** *sah-Lə / chahr-shahm-BAH / pehr-shem-BEH*
Friday / Saturday / Sunday	**Cuma / Cumartesi / Pazar** *joo-MAH / joo-mahr-teh-SİH / pah-ZAHR*
How about the 18th of this month?	**Bu ayın on sekizine ne dersin?** *boo ah-YƏN ohn seh-kih-zih-NEH neh dehr-SİHN?*
Is the (day) of (month) convenient for you?	**(...) (...) uygun mu senin için?** *(...) (...) ooy-GOON moo seh-NİHN ih-CHİHN?*
Is the 5th of February convenient for you?	**Beş Şubat uygun mu senin için?** *behsh shoo-BAHT ooy-GOON moo seh-NİHN ih-CHİHN?*
One / two / three / four / five / six	**bir / iki / üç / dört / beş / altı** *bihr / ih-KİH / üch / dört / behsh / ahl-Tə*
Seven / eight / nine / ten / eleven	**yedi / sekiz / dokuz / on / on bir** *yeh-DİH / seh-KİHZ / doh-KOOZ / ohn / ohn bihr*
Twelve / thirteen / fourteen / fifteen	**on iki / on üç / on dört / on beş** *ohn ih-KİH / ohn üch / ohn dört / ohn behsh*

Sixteen / seventeen / eighteen / nineteen	**on altı / on yedi / on sekiz / on dokuz** *ohn ahl-TƏ / ohn yeh-DİH / ohn seh-KİHZ / ohn doh-KOOZ*
Twenty / twenty-one / twenty-two	**yirmi / yirmi bir / yirmi iki** *yihr-MİH / yihr-MİH bihr / yihr-MİH ih-KİH*
Twenty-three / twenty four / twenty-five	**yirmi üç / yirmi dört / yirmi beş** *yihr-MİH üch / yihr-MİH dört / yihr-MİH behsh*
Twenty-six / twenty-seven	**yirmi altı / yirmi yedi** *yihr-MİH ahl-TƏ / yihr-MİH yeh-DİH*
Twenty-eight / twenty-nine	**yirmi sekiz / yirmi dokuz** *yihr-MİH seh-KİHZ / yihr-MİH doh-KOOZ*
Thirty / thirty-one	**otuz / otuz bir** *oh-TOOZ / oh-TOOZ bihr*
January / February / March	**Ocak / Şubat / Mart** *oh-JAHK / shoo-BAHT / mahrt*
April / May / June	**Nisan / Mayıs / Haziran** *nih-SAHN / mah-YƏS / hah-zih-RAHN*
July / August / September	**Temmuz / Ağustos / Eylül** *tehm-MOOZ / ah-ghoos-TOHS / ehy-LÜL*

October / November / December	**Ekim / Kasım / Aralık** *eh-KİHM / kah-SƏM / ah-rah-LƏK*
Could it be sooner?	**Daha erken olabilir mi?** *dah-DAH ehr-KEHN oh-lah-bih-LİHR mih?*
At one (o'clock) / at two / at three	**(Saat) birde / ikide / üçte** *sah-AHT bihr-DEH /ih-kih-DEH / üch-TEH*
At four (o'clock) / at five / at six	**(Saat) dörtte / beşte / altıda** *sah-AHT dört-TEH / behsh-TEH / ahl-tə-DAH*
At seven (o'clock) / at eight / at nine	**(Saat) yedide / sekizde / dokuzda** *sah-AHT yeh-dih-DEH / seh-kihz-DEH / doh-kooz-DAH*
At ten (o'clock) / at eleven / at twelve	**(Saat) onda / on birde / on ikide** *sah-AHT ohn-DAH / ohn bihr-DEH / ohn ih-kih-DEH*

Don't forget to add **saat** ("clock") at the beginning of the number.

Half past seven	**Yedi buçuk** *yeh-DİH boo-CHOOK*

Just add **buçuk** after the number to say half past that number.

At half past seven	**Yedi buçukta** *yeh-DİH boo-chook-TAH*

7:20 A.M.	**Sabah yediyi yirmi geçe** *sah-BAHH yeh-dih-YİH yihr-MİH geh-CHEH*
6:10 P.M.	**Akşam altıyı on geçe** *ahk-SHAHM ahl-tə-YƏ ohn geh-CHEH*
Quarter till 5	**Beşe on beş kala** *beh-SHEH ohn behsh kah-LAH*
Quarter past 10	**Onu on beş geçe** *oh-NOO ohn behsh geh-CHEH*
Morning	**Sabah** *sah-BAHH*
Afternoon	**Öğleden sonra** *ögh-leh-DEHN sohn-RAH*
Evening	**Akşam** *ahk-SHAHM*
Night	**Gece** *geh-JEH*
What time do we go?	**Ne zaman gidiyoruz?** *neh zah-MAHN gih-dih-yoh-ROOZ?*
What time will you be back?	**Ne zaman geri döneceksin?** *neh zah-MAHN geh-RİH dö-neh-jehk-SİHN?*
Are you ready?	**Hazır mısın?** *hah-ZƏR mə-sən?*

How long will it take?	**Ne kadar sürecek?** *neh kah-DAHR sü-reh-JEHK?*
What time do I come to pick you up?	**Saat kaçta seni almaya geleyim?** *sah-AHT kahch-TAH seh-NİH ahl-mah-YAH geh-leh-YİHM?*
I'm almost done.	**Bitirmek üzereyim.** *bih-tihr-MEHK ü-zeh-reh-YİHM*
Not now.	**Şimdi değil.** *shihm-DİH deh-GHİHL*
Maybe later.	**Belki daha sonra.** *behl-KİH dah-HAH sohn-RAH*
I don't know yet.	**Henüz bilmiyorum.** *heh-NÜZ bihl-mih-yoh-ROOM*
Previously	**Daha önce** *dah-HAH ön-JEH*
Sometime	**Bazen** *bah-ZEHN*
Someday	**Bir gün** *bihr gün*
Always	**Her zaman** *hehr zah-MAHN*
Every day	**Her gün** *hehr gün*

Never	**Hiçbir zaman** *hihch-BİHR zah-MAHN*
Whenever you want.	**Sen ne zaman istersen.** *sehn neh zah-MAHN ihs-tehr-SEHN*
It'll only take a minute.	**Sadece birkaç dakika sürecek.** *sah-deh-JEH bihr-KAHCH dah-kih-KAH sü-reh-JEHK*
Hurry up!	**Acele et!** *ah-jeh-LEH eht!*
Have you finished?	**Bitirdin mi?** *bih-tihr-DİHN mih?*
I've finished.	**Bitirdim.** *bih-tihr-DİHM*
I haven't finished it yet.	**Henüz bitirmedim.** *heh-NÜZ bih-tihr-meh-DİHM*
Is it over?	**Bitti mi?** *biht-TİH mih?*

Hey There! 4

Listen to me!	**Beni dinle!** *beh-NİH dihn-LEH!*
Could you listen to me?	**Beni dinler misin?** *beh-NİH dihn-LEHR mih-sihn?*
Do you hear something?	**Bir şey duyuyor musun?** *bihr shehy doo-yoo-YOHR moo-soon?*
What's that noise?	**O gürültü ne?** *oh gü-rül-TÜ neh?*
What was that noise?	**O gürültü neydi?** *oh gü-rül-TÜ nehy-DİH?*
Don't listen to him.	**Sen onu dinleme.** *sehn oh-NOO dihn-leh-MEH*
Don't ask me a question like that!	**Bana böyle bir soru sorma!** *bah-NAH böy-LEH bihr soh-ROO sohr-MAH!*
I don't want to answer that question.	**Bu soruya cevap vermek istemiyorum.** *boo soh-roo-YAH jeh-VAHP vehr-MEHK ihs-teh-mih-yoh-ROOM*

Can you hear me?	**Beni duyabiliyor musun?** *beh-NİH doo-yah-bih-lih-YOHR moo-soon?*
Did you hear me?	**Beni duydun mu?** *beh-NİH dooy-DOON moo?*
Did you hear what I said?	**Ne dediğimi duydun mu?** *neh de-dih-ghih-MİH dooy-DOON moo?*
I don't want to hear anything about this topic.	**Bu konuda hiç bir şey duymak istemiyorum.** *boo koh-noo-DAH hihch bihr shehy dooy-MAHK ihs-teh-mih-yoh-ROOM*
Don't say things like that!	**Böyle şeyler söyleme!** *böy-LEH shehy-LEHR söy-leh-MEH!*
You shouldn't say things like that.	**Böyle şeyler söylememelisin.** *böy-LEH shehy-LEHR söy-leh-meh-meh-lih-SİHN*
I didn't say anything.	**Bir şey demedim.** *bihr shehy deh-meh-DİHM*
Let's talk in Turkish.	**Hadi Türkçe konuşalım.** *hah-DİH türk-CHEH koh-noo-shah-LƏM*
My Turkish is very good.	**Türkçem bayağı iyi.** *türk-CHEHM bah-ya-GHƏ ih-YİH*

I know very little Turkish.	**Çok az Türkçe biliyorum.** *chohk ahz türk-CHEH bih-lih-yoh-ROOM*
Let's talk about it later.	**Hadi bunu sonra konuşalım.** *hah-DİH boo-NOO sohn-RAH koh-noo-shah-LƏM*
I don't want to talk.	**Konuşmak istemiyorum.** *koh-noosh-MAHK ihs-teh-mih-yoh-ROOM*
I don't want to talk to you.	**Seninle konuşmak istemiyorum.** *seh-nihn-LEH koh-noosh-MAHK ihs-teh-mih-yoh-ROOM*
I don't want to talk about this.	**Bu konuda konuşmak istemiyorum.** *boo koh-noo-DAH koh-noosh-MAHK ihs-teh-mih-yoh-ROOM*
Can we talk about this later?	**Bu konuyu sonra konuşabilir miyiz?** *boo koh-noo-YOO sohn-RAH koh-noo-shah-bih-LİHR mih-yihz?*
These are all excuses.	**Bunların hepsi bahane.** *boon-lah-RƏN hehp-SİH bah-hah-NEH*
What kind of excuse is that!	**Ne biçim bir bahane bu!** *neh bih-CHİHM bihr bah-hah-NEH boo!*

Stop complaining.	**Şikayet etmeyi bırak.** *shi-kah-YEHT eht-meh-YİH bə-RAHK*
Don't talk so loudly!	**Yüksek sesle konuşma!** *yük-SEHK sehs-LEH koh-noosh-MAH!*
Speak up.	**Biraz yüksek sesle konuş.** *bih-RAHZ yük-SEHK sehs-LEH koh-NOOSH*
Speak more slowly, please.	**Biraz yavaş konuş, lütfen.** *bih-RAHZ yah-VAHSH koh-NOOSH, lüt-FEHN*
Can you say it again?	**Tekrar eder misin?** *tehk-RAHR eh-DEHR mih-sihn?*
Do you understand?	**Anlıyor musun?** *ahn-lə-YOHR moo-soon?*
Do you understand me?	**Beni anlıyor musun?** *beh-NİH ahn-lə-YOHR moo-soon?*
You don't understand me.	**Beni anlamıyorsun.** *beh-NİH ahn-lah-mə-yohr-SOON*
I don't understand you.	**Seni anlamıyorum.** *seh-NİH ahn-lah-mə-yoh-ROOM*
What did you say?	**Ne dedin?** *neh deh-DİHN?*

If you have not heard what was said, you can also say "**Efendim?**" which could be roughly translated as "I beg your pardon?" You would pronounce it as "*eh-fehn-dihm.*"

I didn't mean to say that.	**Öyle demek istemedim.** *öy-LEH deh-MEHK ihs-teh-meh-DİHM*
I didn't say anything like that.	**Ben öyle bir şey demedim.** *behn öy-LEH bihr shehy deh-meh-DİHM*
I didn't tell anyone.	**Kimseye bir şey söylemedim.** *kihm-seh-YEH bihr shehy söy-leh-meh-DİHM*
I won't tell anyone.	**Kimseye bir şey söylemem.** *kihm-seh-YEH bihr shehy söy-leh-MEHM*
Don't mention this to anyone!	**Bundan kimseye bahsetme!** *boon-DAHN kihm-seh-YEH bahh-seht-MEH!*
I won't mention this to anyone.	**Bundan kimseye bahsetmem.** *boon-DAHN kihm-seh-YEH bahh-seht-MEHM*

Look at That 5

Look!	**Bak!** *bahk!*
Look at this!	**Buna bak!** *boo-NAH bahk!*
Look at that!	**Şuna bak!** *shoo-NAH bahk!*
Don't look.	**Bakma.** *bahk-MAH*
Can you see it?	**Onu görebiliyor musun?** *oh-NOO gö-reh-bih-lih-YOHR moo-soon?*
Did you see it?	**Onu gördün mü?** *oh-NOO gör-DÜN mü?*
Don't you see?	**Görmüyor musun?** *gör-mü-YOHR moo-soon?*
I can't see anything.	**Hiç bir şey göremiyorum.** *hihch bihr shehy gö-reh-mih-yoh-ROOM*

I can see it clearly.	**Çok net görebiliyorum.** *chohk neht gö-reh-bih-lih-yoh-ROOM*
I can't believe what I saw.	**Gördüklerime inanamıyorum.** *gör-dük-leh-rih-MEH ih-nah-nah-mə-yoh-ROOM*
I saw it.	**Onu gördüm.** *oh-NOO gör-DÜM*
I didn't see it.	**Onu görmedim.** *oh-NOO gör-meh-DİHM*
I don't want to see it.	**Onu görmek istemiyorum.** *oh-NOO gör-MEHK ihs-teh-mih-yoh-ROOM*
Have you seen Can?	**Canı gördün mü?** *jah-NƏ gör-DÜN mü?*
When can I see you?	**Seni ne zaman görebilirim?** *seh-NİH neh zah-MAHN gö-reh-bih-lih-RİHM?*

I want to see you soon.	**En kısa zamanda seni görmek istiyorum.** *ehn kə-SAH zah-mahn-DAH seh-NİH gör-MEHK ihs-tih-yoh-ROOM*
I don't want to see you anymore.	**Seni görmek istemiyorum artık.** *seh-NİH gör-MEHK ihs-teh-mih-yoh-ROOM ahr-TƏK*
I really want to see you.	**Seni görmeyi çok istiyorum.** *seh-NİH gör-meh-YİH chohk ihs-tih-yoh-ROOM*
I'm going to see Can next week.	**Gelecek hafta Canı göreceğim.** *geh-le-JEHK hahf-TAH jah-NƏ gö-reh-jeh-GHİHM*

Coming & Going 6

Come here.	**Buraya gel.** *boo-rah-YAH gehl*
Come over to my place.	**Benim eve gel.** *beh-NİHM eh-VEH gehl*
I'll be there in a moment.	**Birazdan orada olurum.** *bih-rahz-DAHN oh-rah-DAH oh-loo-ROOM*
I'll be there soon.	**En kısa zamanda orada olacağım.** *ehn kə-SAH zah-mahn-DAH oh-rah-DAH oh-lah-jah-GHƏM*
Come later.	**Daha sonra gel.** *dah-HAH sohn-RAH gehl*
Can you come?	**Gelebilir misin?** *geh-leh-bih-LİHR mih-sihn?*
Come with us.	**Bizimle gel.** *bih-zihm-LEH gehl*
I'm coming, wait for me.	**Geliyorum, bekle beni.** *geh-lih-yoh-ROOM, behk-LEH beh-NİH*

He's / She's coming here.	**O buraya geliyor.** *oh boo-rah-YAH geh-lih-YOHR*

Remember, in Turkish **o** is used for both "he" and "she," so this sentence can be used for either gender.

I'll go soon.	**Birazdan gideceğim.** *bih-rahz-DAHN gih-deh-jeh-GHİHM*
I can go.	**Gidebilirim.** *gih-deh-bih-lih-RİHM*
I think I can go.	**Sanırım gidebilirim.** *sah-nə-RƏM gih-deh-bih-lih-RİHM*
I can't go.	**Gidemem.** *gih-deh-MEHM*
I want to go.	**Gitmek istiyorum.** *giht-MEHK ihs-tih-yoh-ROOM*
I want to go to Istanbul.	**İstanbul'a gitmek istiyorum.** *İHS-tahn-boolah giht-MEHK ihs-tih-yoh-ROOM*
I really want to go.	**Gerçekten gitmek istiyorum.** *gehr-chehk-TEHN giht-MEHK ihs-tih-yoh-ROOM*
I don't want to go.	**Gitmek istemiyorum.** *giht-MEHK ihs-teh-mih-yoh-ROOM*
I really don't want to go.	**Gitmeyi hiç istemiyorum.** *giht-meh-YİH hihch ihs-teh-mih-yoh-ROOM*

You are going, aren't you?	**Gidiyorsun, değil mi?** *gih-dih-yohr-SOON, deh-GHİHL mih?*

In everyday language, instead of **değil mi**, you can say **di mi** as the Turkish natives often do. You pronounce it "*dih mih.*"

You went, didn't you?	**Gittin, değil mi?** *giht-TİHN, deh-GHİHL mih?*
I'm going.	**Gidiyorum.** *gih-dih-yoh-ROOM*
I'm not going.	**Gitmiyorum.** *giht-mih-yoh-ROOM*
You'll go, won't you?	**Gideceksin, değil mi?** *gih-deh-jehk-SİHN, deh-GHİL mih?*
I went.	**Gittim.** *giht-TİHM*
I didn't go.	**Gitmedim.** *giht-meh-DİHM*
I will go.	**Gideceğim.** *gih-deh-jeh-GHİHM*
I will not go.	**Gitmeyeceğim.** *giht-meh-yeh-jeh-GHİHM*
Don't go!	**Gitme!** *giht-MEH!*

Don't go yet!	**Henüz gitme!** *heh-NÜZ giht-MEH!*
I have to go.	**Gitmeliyim.** *giht-meh-lih-YİHM*
I must go now.	**Şimdi gitmeliyim.** *shihm-DİH giht-meh-lih-YİHM*
May I go?	**Gidebilir miyim?** *gih-deh-bih-LİHR mih-yihm?*
Shall we go?	**Gidelim mi?** *gih-deh-LİHM mih?*
Let's go!	**Hadi gidelim!** *hah-DİH gih-deh-LİHM!*
Let's leave here.	**Hadi gidelim burdan.** *hah-DİH gih-deh-LİHM boor-DAHN*
I'm leaving shortly.	**Birazdan gidiyorum.** *bih-rahz-DAHN gih-dih-yoh-ROOM*
Stay here.	**Burada kal.** *boo-rah-DAH kahl*

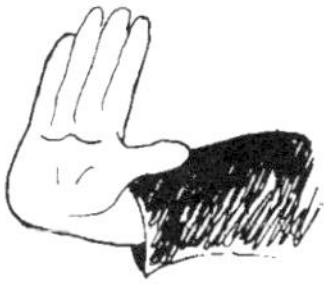

Where are you going? **Nereye gidiyorsun?**
neh-reh-YEH gih-dih-yohr-SOON?

Where are you coming from? **Nereden geliyorsun?**
neh-reh-DEHN geh-lih-yohr-SOON?

Where I go doesn't concern you! **Nereye gittiğim seni ilgilendirmez!**
neh-reh-YEH giht-tih-GHİHM seh-NİH ihl-gih-lehn-dihr-MEHZ!

Go slowly. **Yavaş git.**
yah-VAHSH giht

Eat, Drink & Be Merry 7

Are you hungry?	**Aç mısın?** *AHCH mə-sən?*
I'm hungry.	**Acıktım.** *ah-jək-TƏM*
I'm starving.	**Açlıktan ölüyorum.** *ahch-lək-TAHN ö-lü-yoh-ROOM*
I am very hungry.	**Karnım zil çalıyor.** *kahr-NƏM zihl chah-lə-YOHR*

This literally means "my stomach is ringing a bell."

I am as hungry as a fox.	**Kurt gibi acıktım.** *koort gih-BİH ah-jək-TƏM*

This is another colloquial saying meaning "I'm starving."

Let's go eat something.	**Hadi bir şeyler yemeye gidelim.** *hah-DİH bihr shehy-LEHR yeh-meh-YEH gih-deh-LİHM*
I've eaten already.	**Ben zaten yedim.** *behn zah-TEHN yeh-DİHM*
I'm not hungry.	**Aç değilim.** *ahch deh-ghih-LİHM*

I haven't eaten anything yet.	**Henüz bir şey yemedim.** *heh-NÜZ bihr-shehy yeh-meh-DİHM*
Do you want to eat something?	**Bir şeyler yemek ister misin?** *bihr-shehy-LEHR yeh-MEHK ihs-TEHR mih-sihn?*
What do you want to eat?	**Ne yemek istersin?** *neh yeh-MEHK ihs-tehr-SİHN?*
I don't want to eat anything.	**Bir şey yemek istemiyorum.** *bihr-shehy yeh-MEHK ihs-teh-mih-yoh-ROOM*
Do you want some more?	**Biraz daha ister misin?** *bih-RAHZ dah-HAH ihs-TEHR mih-sihn?*
Yes, please.	**Evet, lütfen.** *eh-VEHT, lüt-FEHN*
No, thanks.	**Hayır, teşekkürler.** *hah-YƏR, teh-shehk-kür-LEHR*
I'm thirsty.	**Susadım.** *soo-sah-DƏM*
Do you want something to drink?	**İçecek bir şey ister misin?** *ih-cheh-JEHK bihr shehy ihs-TEHR mih-sihn?*
What do you want to drink?	**Ne içmek istersin?** *neh ihch-MEHK ihs-tehr-SİHN?*

(Can I get) a glass of water?	**Bir bardak su (alabilir miyim)?** *bihr bahr-DAHK soo (ah-lah-bih-LİHR mih-yihm)?*
(I would like) a glass of water.	**Bir bardak su (rica ediyorum).** *bihr bahr-DAHK soo (rih-JAH eh-dih-yoh-ROOM)*
A bottled water.	**Bir şişe su.** *Bihr shih-SHEH soo*
A bottled mineral water.	**Bir şişe maden suyu.** *bihr shih-SHEH mah-DEHN soo-YOO*
A bottled sparkling mineral water.	**Bir şişe maden sodası.** *bihr shih-SHEH mah-DEHN soh-dah-SƏ*
A glass of orange juice.	**Bir bardak portakal suyu.** *bihr bahr-DAHK pohr-tah-KAHL soo-YOO*
A glass of lemonade.	**Bir bardak limonata.** *bihr bahr-DAHK lih-moh-nah-TAH*

A glass of tea. **Bir bardak çay.**
bihr bahr-DAHK chahy

Tea is prepared without sugar and is served with cubes of sugar on the saucer. Or it may come with a small sugar bowl so you can add sugar using your teaspoon.

A cup of coffee. **Bir fincan kahve.**
bihr fihn-JAHN kahh-VEH

Unless it's otherwise stated, coffee is prepared without sugar.

With sugar **Şekerli**
sheh-kehr-LİH

Medium sweet **Orta şekerli**
ohr-TAH sheh-kehr-LİH

Really sweet **Bol şekerli**
bohl sheh-kehr-LİH

Without sugar **Şekersiz**
sheh-kehr-SİHZ

A beer. **Bir bira**
bihr bih-RAH

A glass of wine. **Bir kadeh şarap.**
bihr kah-DEHH shah-RAHP

A bottle of champagne. **Bir şişe şampanya.**
bihr shih-SHEH shahm-pahn-YAH

A glass of champagne. **Bir kadeh şampanya.**
bihr kah-DEHH shahm-pahn-YAH

A glass of rakı.	**Bir kadeh rakı.** *bihr kah-DEHH rah-Kə*

Rakı is a clear brandy, made from distilled grapes, flavored with anise. It's the most consumed alcoholic beverage in Turkey and has a high alcohol content—up to 50%. It's consumed mixed with water. It's colorless but when mixed with water, it turns a milky white color. **Rakı** is usually served along with **meze** (several small-sized appetizers).

A glass of gin.	**Bir kadeh viski.** *bihr kah-DEHH vihs-KİH*
A glass of vodka.	**Bir kadeh votka.** *bihr kah-DEHH voht-KAH*
A table for four, please.	**Dört kişilik bir masa, lütfen.** *dört kih-shih-LİHK bihr mah-SAH, lüt-FEHN*
Can I see the menu?	**Menüyü görebilir miyim?** *meh-nü-YÜ gö-reh-bih-LİHR mih-yihm?*
We haven't decided yet.	**Henüz karar vermedik.** *heh-NÜZ kah-RAHR vehr-meh-DİHK*
Can you give us a few minutes?	**Bize birkaç dakika verir misin?** *bih-ZEH bihr-KAHCH dah-kih-KAH veh-RİHR mih-sihn?*
I'm ready to order.	**Sipariş için hazırım.** *sih-pah-RİHSH ih-CHİHN hah-zə-RƏM*

We're ready to order. **Sipariş için hazırız.**
sih-pah-RİHSH ih-CHİHN hah-zə–RƏZ

Can I get the bill? **Hesabı alabilir miyim?**
heh-sah-BƏ ah-lah-bih-LİHR mih-yihm?

Can I use my credit card? **Kredi kartımı kullanabilir miyim?**
kreh-DİH kahr-tə-MƏ kool-lah-nah-bih-LİHR mih-yihm?

Keep the change. **Üstü kalsın.**
üs-TÜ kahl-SƏN

I don't want to drink. **İçmek istemiyorum.**
ihch-MEHK ihs-teh-mih-yoh-ROOM

I won't drink. **İçmeyeceğim.**
ihch-meh-yeh-jeh-GHİHM

Come on, drink a little bit more. **Hadi, biraz daha iç.**
hah-DİH, bih-RAHZ dah-HAH ihch

The common expression "**hadi**" is further explained in Chapter 1. In this sentence, it reflects insistence.

This tastes too weird. **Bunun tadı çok garip.**
boo-NOON tah-DƏ chohk gah-RİHP

I think this has gone bad. **Sanırım bu bozulmuş.**
sah-nə-RƏM boo boh-zool-MOOSH

This looks delicious. **Bu çok leziz görünüyor.**
boo chohk leh-ZİHZ gö-rü-nü-YOHR

This tastes delicious! **(Valla) bu çok lezzetli!**
(vahl-LAH) boo chohk lehz-zeht-LİH!

Valla is a word of Arabic origin which means "I swear on God." It's not used in religious contexts only, though. In colloquial Turkish, **valla** is used very commonly to mean "really." So the sentence above, with the **valla** included, could be translated as "this really tastes good."

How about some dinner with me? **Benimle yemeğe gitmeye ne dersin?**
beh-nihm-LEH yeh-meh-GHEH giht-meh-YEH neh dehr-SİHN?

Is the meal ready? **Yemek hazır mı?**
yeh-MEHK hah-zər MƏ?

In Turkish culture, eating is beyond grabbing a bite for nourishment. It's the time when the whole family gathers at the table. The food is always prepared with utmost care. Although they do go to restaurants occasionally, Turkish people mostly eat home-cooked meals.

Yes, it's ready. **Evet, hazır.**
eh-VEHT, hah-ZƏR

That looks delicious. **Çok leziz görünüyor.**
chohk leh-ZİHZ gö-rü-nü-YOHR

It smells really good. **Valla mis gibi kokuyor.**
vahl-LAH mihs gih-BİH koh-koo-YOHR

May I have some more? **Biraz daha alabilir miyim?**
bih-RAHZ dah-HAH ah-lah-bih-LİHR mih-yihm?

Do you want more?	**Biraz daha ister misin?** *bih-RAHZ dah-HAH ihs-TEHR mih-sihn?*
Just a little, please.	**Çok az, lütfen.** *chohk ahz, lüt-FEHN*
A little more.	**Biraz daha.** *bih-RAHZ dah-HAH*
Enough?	**Yeterli mi?** *yeh-tehr-LİH mih?*
This is enough.	**Bu kadar yeterli.** *boo kah-DAHR yeh-tehr-LİH*
What's the name of this?	**Bunun adı ne?** *boo-NOON ah-DƏ neh?*
Taste it once.	**Bir kez tadına bak.** *bihr kehz tah-də-NAH bahk*
I can't eat this.	**Bunu yiyemem ben.** *boo-NOO yih-yeh-MEHM behn*
Is it spicy?	**Acı mı bu?** *ah-JƏ mə boo?*
I don't like spicy food.	**Acılı yemekleri sevmem.** *ah-jə-LƏ yeh-mehk-leh-RİH sehv-MEHM*
I'm allergic to spicy food.	**Acılı yemeklere alerjim var.** *ah-jə-LƏ yeh-mehk-leh-REH ah-lehr-ZHİHM vahr*

This is too spicy.	**Bu çok acı.** *boo chohk ah-JƏ*
My mouth is on fire.	**Ağzım yanıyor.** *ahgh-ZƏM yah-nə-YOHR*

Yum!	**Nefis!** *neh-FİHS!*
The food is great.	**Yemek harika olmuş.** *yeh-MEHK hah-rih-KAH ohl-MOOSH*
Can you bring me a (fork / spoon / knife / napkin)?	**Lütfen bana bir (çatal / kaşık / bıçak / peçete) getirir misin?** *lüt-FEHN bah-NAH bihr (chah-TAHL / kah-SHƏK / bə-CHAHK / peh-cheh-TEH) geh-tih-RİHR mih-sihn?*
I didn't like the taste of this.	**Bunun tadını hiç beğenmedim.** *boo-NOON tah-də-NƏ hihch beh-ghehn-meh-DİHM*

How do you eat this? **Bu nasıl yenir?**
boo nah-SəL yeh-NİHR?

Bless your hands. **Eline sağlık.**
eh-lih-NEH sahgh-LəK

This is said to someone who cooked a meal for you.

Bon appetit. **Afiyet olsun.**
ah-fih-YEHT ohl-SOON

This is said as a response when someone has thanked you for a meal you cooked, or when you see someone eating a meal.

I Like It! 8

I like this.	**Bunu beğendim.** *boo-NOO beh-ghehn-DİHM*
I like it a lot.	**Bunu çok beğendim.** *boo-NOO chohk beh-ghehn-DİHM*
I didn't like it at all.	**Bunu hiç beğenmedim.** *boo-NOO hihch beh-ghehn-meh-DİHM*
I hate it.	**Bundan nefret ettim.** *boon-DAHN nehf-REHT eht-TİHM*

This is seldom used. Instead, "I didn't like it at all" is used for situations of strong dislike.

I want... (noun)	**... istiyorum** *ihs-tih-yoh-ROOM*
I want ice cream.	**Dondurma istiyorum.** *dohn-door-MAH ihs-tih-yoh-ROOM*
I don't want... (noun)	**... istemiyorum** *ihs-teh-mih-yoh-ROOM*
I don't want ice cream.	**Dondurma istemiyorum.** *dohn-door-MAH ihs-teh-mih-yoh-ROOM*

I don't want to... (verb) — ... **istemiyorum**
ihs-teh-mih-yoh-ROOM

I don't want to eat ice cream. — **Dondurma yemek istemiyorum.**
dohn-door-MAH yeh-MEHK ihs-teh-mih-yoh-ROOM

The formula for constructing "I don't want to..." sentences is the infinitive form of the verb + **istemiyorum**:

Ders calışmak (to study) + **istemiyorum** = I don't want to study.
Konuşmak (to talk) + **istemiyorum** = I don't want to talk.

I don't have to deal with this. — **Bununla uğraşmak zorunda değilim.**
boo-noon-LAH oogh-rahsh-MAHK zoh-roon-DAH deh-ghih-LİHM

I don't want to deal with this. — **Bununla uğraşmak istemiyorum.**
boo-noon-LAH oogh-rahsh-MAHK ihs-teh-mih-yoh-ROOM

I'm pleased to hear that. — **Bunu duyduğuma sevindim.**
boo-NOO dooy-doo-ghoo-MAH seh-vihn-DİHM

I'm glad to know that. — **Bunu öğrendiğime sevindim.**
boo-NOO ögh-rehn-dih-ghih-MEH seh-vihn-DİHM

I'm busy. — **Meşgulüm.**
mehsh-goo-LÜM

I'm happy. — **Mutluyum.**
moot-loo-YOOM

I'm not happy. — **Mutsuzum.**
moot-soo-ZOOM

I'm sad. — **Üzgünüm.**
üz-gü-NÜM

I'm fine. — **İyiyim.**
ih-yih-YİHM

I'm afraid. — **Korkuyorum.**
kohr-koo-yoh-ROOM

I'm sick of this. — **Bıktım bundan.**
bək-TƏM boon-DAHN

I'm sick of you. — **Bıktım senden.**
bək-TƏM sehn-DEHN

I'm sick of dealing with this.	**Bununla uğraşmaktan bıktım.** *boo-noon-LAH oogh-rahsh-mahk-TAHN bək-TƏM*
I'm mad at you.	**Sana kızgınım.** *sah-NAH kəz-gə-NƏM*
I'm offended by you.	**Sana dargınım.** *sah-NAH dahr-gə-NƏM*
I'm confused.	**Kafam karmakarışık.** *kah-FAHM kahr-mah-kah-rə-SHƏK*
I'm going crazy.	**Deli oluyorum.** *deh-LİH oh-loo-yoh-ROOM*
You are driving me crazy!	**Beni deli ediyorsun!** *beh-NİH deh-lih eh-dih-yohr-SOON!*
I'm ready.	**Hazırım.** *hah-zə-RƏM*
I'm tired.	**Yorgunum.** *yohr-goo-NOOM*
I'm sleepy.	**Uykum var.** *ooy-KOOM vahr*
I'm shocked.	**Şaşırdım.** *shah-shər-DƏM*
I'm bored.	**Sıkıldım.** *sə-kəl-DƏM*

I feel sick.	**Kendimi rahatsız hissediyorum.** *kehn-dih-MİH rah-haht-SƏZ hihs-seh-dih-yoh-ROOM*
I'm disappointed.	**Hayal kırıklığına uğradım.** *hah-YAHL kə-rək-lə-ghə-NAH oogh-rah-DƏM*
I am disappointed in you.	**Beni hayal kırıklığına uğrattın.** *beh-NİH hah-YAHL kə-rək-lə-ghə-NAH oogh-raht-TƏN*
I'm worried about you.	**Senin için endişeleniyorum.** *seh-NİHN ih-CHİHN ehn-dih-sheh-leh-nih-yoh-ROOM*
Can you do it?	**Bunu yapabilir misin?** *boo-NOO yah-pah-bih-LİHR mih-sihn?*
I can do it.	**Yapabilirim.** *yah-pah-bih-lih-RİHM*
I can't do it.	**Yapamam.** *yah-pah-MAHM*
I'll do it.	**Yapacağım.** *yah-pah-jah-GHƏM*
I won't do it.	**Yapmayacağım.** *yahp-mah-yah-jah-GHƏM*

I've got to do it.	**Yapmalıyım.** *yahp-mah-lə-YƏM*
I did.	**Yaptım.** *yahp-TƏM*
I didn't.	**Yapmadim.** *yahp-mah-DƏM*
Sorry.	**Üzgünüm.** *üz-gü-NÜM*
I understand.	**Anlıyorum.** *ahn-lə-yoh-ROOM*
I know.	**Biliyorum.** *bih-lih-yoh-ROOM*
I lost my chance.	**Şansımı kaybettim.** *shahn-sə-MƏ kahy-beht-TİHM*
You lost your chance.	**Şansını kaybettin.** *shahn-sə-NƏ kahy-beht-TİHN*

Fighting & Curses 9

What do you want? **Ne istiyorsun (ya)?**
neh ihs-tih-yohr-SOON (yah)?

Be and **ya** are words that have no literal meanings. They are used at the end of a sentence to express irritation or anger. They don't change the meaning of a sentence, they only add emphasis. They're used in colloquial speaking only—not in proper Turkish.

Don't look at me like that! **Bana öyle bakma!**
bah-NAH öy-LEH bahk-MAH!

What are you staring at! **Ne bakıyorsun (be)!**
neh bah-kə-yohr-SOON (beh)!

What did you say! **Ne dedin sen!**
neh deh-DİHN-sehn!

Who do you think you're talking to? — **Kiminle konuştuğunu zannediyorsun sen?**
kih-mihn-LEH koh-noosh-too-ghoo-NOO zahn-neh-dih-yohr-SOON sehn?

Who do you think you are? — **Kim olduğunu zannediyorsun sen?**
kihm ohl-doo-ghoo-NOO zahn-neh-dih-yohr-SOON sehn?

Do you know who I am? — **Sen benim kim olduğumu biliyor musun?**
sehn beh-NİHM kihm ohl-doo-ghoo-MOO bih-lih-yohr-moo-SOON?

Come here so I can teach you manners! — **Gel de göstereyim!**
gehl deh gös-teh-reh-YİHM!

This is a sarcastic remark showing an intent to fight. It literally means "come so I can show you."

Don't mess around with me! — **Benimle uğraşma!**
beh-nihm-LEH oogh-rahsh-MAH!

Don't do it! — **Yapma (be)!**
yahp-MAH (beh)!

Shut up! — **Kes sesini (be)!**
kehs seh-sih-NİH (beh)!

What do you think you're doing! — **Ne yaptığını zannediyorsun sen!**
neh yahp-tə-ghə-Nə zahn-neh-dih-yohr-SOON sehn!

You're hurting me! **Canımı acıtıyorsun!**
jah-nə-MƏ ah-cə-tə-yohr-SOON!

It seems you want to fight! **Kavga etmek istiyorsun galiba!**
kahv-GAH eht-MEHK ihs-tih-yohr-SOON gah-lih-BAH!

A sarcastic remark to express that someone is pushing your buttons.

I am going to kill you. **Seni öldüreceğim.**
seh-NİH öl-dü-reh-jeh-GHİHM

I kill you. **Seni öldürürüm.**
seh-NİH öl-dü-rü-RÜM

Both the future and the present tenses can be used interchangeably. These phrases are often used in Turkish fights, but not meant literally.

Don't hit me! **Vurma!**
voor-MAH!

Stop! **Dur!**
door!

Don't do it again! **Bir daha yapma!**
bihr dah-HAH yahp-MAH!

You deserve this.	**Bunu hak ediyorsun.** *boo-NOO hahk-eh-dih-yohr-SOON*
I didn't deserve this.	**Bunu hak etmedim.** *boo-NOO hahk eht-meh-DİHM*
You deserved this.	**Bunu hak ettin.** *boo-NOO hahk eht-TİHN*
You're right.	**Haklısın.** *hahk-lə-SƏN*
The mistake was mine.	**Hata benimdi.** *hah-TAH beh-nihm-DİH*
It was my fault.	**Suç benimdi.** *sooch beh-nihm-DİH*
Excuse me.	**Affedersin.** *ah-feh-dehr-SİHN*
I'm sorry.	**Özür dilerim.** *ö-ZÜR dih-leh-RİHM*
Forgive me.	**Affet beni.** *ahf-FEHT beh-NİH*
I forgive you.	**Seni affediyorum.** *seh-NİH ahf-feh-dih-yoh-ROOM*
You're stupid.	**Sen aptalsın.** *sehn ahp-tahl-SƏN*

What you're doing is stupid. — **Yaptığın sey çok aptalca.**
yahp-tə-GHƏN shehy chohk ahp-tahl-JAH

Liar! — **Yalancı!**
yah-lahn-JƏ!

Don't talk so much! — **Çok konuşma (be)!**
chohk koh-noosh-MAH (beh)!

Come to your senses! — **Kendine gel!**
kehn-dih-NEH gehl!

Bitch! — **Orospu!**
oh-rohs-POO!

It's extremely rude and offensive to call someone anything other than his or her name. Keep in mind that especially insulting a woman reflects very poorly on the speaker.

Son of a bitch! — **Orospu çocuğu!**
oh-rohs-POO choh-joo-GHOO!

Bastard! — **Piç!**
pihch!

This is a very offensive remark since it's expected by Turkish custom to conceive children only after marriage. So this is an insult aimed at the person's family, which would be extremely rude. Insulting someone's mom, sister, or (especially) wife is a big no-no in Turkey and might escalate to fighting.

Faggot! — **İbne!**
ihb-NEH!

Go to hell!	**Canın cehenneme!** *jah-NƏN jeh-hehn-neh-MEH!*
Fuck off!	**Siktir git!** *sihk-TİHR giht!*

Fuck you!	**Seni sikiyim!** *seh-NİH sih-kih-YİHM!*
Damn it!	**Lanet olsun!** *lah-NEHT ohl-SOON!*
God damn it!	**Allah kahretsin!** *ahl-LAHH kahh-reht-SİHN!*
Take your hands off of me!	**Çek ellerini üstümden!** *chehk ehl-leh-rih-NİH üs-tüm-DEHN!*
Don't touch me!	**Dokunma bana!** *doh-koon-MAH bah-NAH!*
Don't think that I'm a fool!	**Aptal olduğumu zannetme!** *ahp-TAHL ohl-doo-ghoo-MOO zahn-neht-MEH!*

Going Out 10

Would you like to hang out together this weekend?	**Bu hafta sonu beraber takılalım mı?** *boo hahf-TAH soh-NOO beh-rah-BEHR tah-kə-lah-LƏM mə?*
Would you like to hang out together tonight?	**Bu akşam beraber takılalım mı?** *boo ahk-SHAHM beh-rah-BEHR tah-kə-lah-LƏM mə?*
I'm bored, let's do something.	**Canım sıkılıyor, hadi bir şeyler yapalım.** *jah-NƏM sə-kə-lə-YOHR, hah-DİH bihr shehy-LEHR yah-pah-LƏM*
Okay, what shall we do?	**Tamam, ne yapalım?** *tah-MAHM, neh yah-pah-LƏM?*
We can go dancing.	**Dans etmeye gidebiliriz.** *dahns eht-meh-YEH gih-deh-bih-lih-RİHZ*
Let's go to a nightclub.	**Hadi diskoya gidelim.** *hah-DİH dihs-koh-YAH gih-deh-LİHM*

Would you like to have dinner with me tonight?
Bugün benimle akşam yemeğine çıkmak ister misin?
boo-GÜN beh-nihm-LEH ahk-SHAHM yeh-meh-ghih-NEH chək-MAHK ihs-TEHR mih-sihn?

Do you want to go to a movie tonight?
Bu akşam benimle sinemaya gitmek ister misin?
boo ahk-SHAHM beh-nihm-LEH sih-neh-mah-YAH giht-MEHK ihs-TEHR mih-sihn?

Let's go to a movie tonight.
Hadi sinemaya gidelim bu akşam.
hah-DİH sih-neh-mah-YAH gih-deh-LİHM boo ahk-SHAHM

What time will you be ready?
Saat kaçta hazır olursun?
sah-AHT kahch-TAH hah-ZƏR oh-loor-SOON?

I'll be ready at 8:00.
Saat sekizde hazır olurum.
sah-AHT seh-kihz-DEH hah-ZƏR oh-loo-ROOM

I'll pick you up at 8:00 this evening.
Seni bu akşam saat sekizde almaya geleceğim.
seh-NİH boo ahk-SHAHM sah-AHT seh-kihz-DEH ahl-mah-YAH geh-leh-jeh-GHİHM

Are you having fun?
Eğleniyor musun?
ehgh-leh-nih-YOHR moo-soon?

Yes, I'm having a lot of fun. **Evet çok eğleniyorum.**
eh-VEHT chohk ehgh-leh-nih-yoh-ROOM

This place is fun. **Burası çok eğlenceli.**
boo-rah-SƏ chohk ehgh-lehn-jeh-LİH

No, I don't like this place much. **Hayır, burayı pek sevmedim.**
hah-YƏR, boo-rah-YƏ pehk sehv-meh-DİHM

Can we go to another place? **Başka bir yere gidebilir miyiz?**
bahsh-KAH bihr yeh-REH gih-deh-bih-LİHR mih-yihz?

Let's go somewhere else. **Hadi başka bir yere gidelim.**
hah-DİH bahsh-KAH bihr yeh-REH gih-deh-LİHM

I'm going to get something to drink. **Bara içki almaya gidiyorum.**
bah-RAH ihch-KİH ahl-mah-YAH gih-dih-yoh-ROOM

You'd say this when heading to get an alcoholic drink from a bartender, not when going to the store or the kitchen to get a beverage.

Do you want something to drink? **İçecek bir şey ister misin?**
ih-cheh-JEHK bihr shehy ihs-TEHR mih-sihn?

Can I buy you a drink? **Sana bir içki ısmarlayabilir miyim?**
sah-NAH bihr ihch-KİH əs-mahr-lah-yah-bih-LİHR mih-yihm?

Can I sit next to you?	**Yanına oturabilir miyim?** *yah-n?-NAH oh-too-rah-bih-LİHR mih-yihm?*
Is someone sitting here?	**Burada oturan biri var mı?** *boo-rah-DAH oh-too-RAHN bih-RİH vahr mə?*
May I sit down?	**Oturabilir miyim?** *oh-too-rah-bih-LİHR mih-yihm?*
Please go ahead, sit down.	**Buyurun, oturun.** *boo-yoo-ROON, oh-too-ROON*
Do you come here often?	**Buraya sık sık gelir misin?** *boo-rah-YAH sək sək geh-LİHR mih-sihn?*
The music is too loud.	**Müzik çok yüksek.** *mü-ZİHK chohk yük-SEHK*
What's your name?	**İsmin ne?** *ihs-MİHN neh?*
My name is Can.	**İsmim Can.** *ihs-MİHM jahn*
Did you come here alone?	**Buraya yalnız mı geldin?** *boo-rah-YAH yahl-NƏZ mə gehl-DİHN?*
Yes I came here alone.	**Evet yalnız geldim.** *eh-VEHT yahl-NƏZ gehl-DİHM*

No, I came with my friends.	**Hayır, arkadaşlarımla geldim.** *hah-YƏR, ahr-kah-dahsh-LAH-rəm-lah gehl-DİHM*
Where are you from?	**Nerelisin?** *neh-reh-lih-SİHN?*
How long have you been in Turkey?	**Kaç senedir Türkiyedesin?** *kahch seh-neh-DİHR tür-kih-yeh-deh-SİHN?*
Do you like Turkish guys?	**Türk erkeklerinden hoşlanır mısın?** *türk ehr-kehk-leh-rihn-DEHN hohsh-lah-NƏR mə-sən?*
Do you like Turkish girls?	**Türk kızlarından hoşlanır mısın?** *türk kəz-lah-rən-DAHN hohsh-lah-NƏR mə-sən?*
I've never met someone Turkish before.	**Daha önce hiç bir Türkle karşılaşmamıştım.** *dah-HAH ön-JEH hihch bihr Türk-LEH kahr-shə-lahsh-mah-məsh-TƏM*
How old are you?	**Kaç yaşındasın?** *kahch yah-shən-dah-SƏN?*
Are you a student?	**Öğrenci misin?** *ögh-rehn-JİH mih-sihn?*

Where do you work? **Nerede çalışıyorsun?**
neh-reh-DEH chah-lə-shə-yohr-SOON?

What do you do in your spare time? **Boş zamanlarında ne yaparsın?**
bohsh zah-mahn-lah-rən-DAH neh yah-pahr-SƏN?

What kind of music do you like? **Ne tür müzikten hoşlanırsın?**
neh tür mü-zihk-TEHN hohsh-lah-nər-SƏN?

I love this song. **Bu şarkıyı çok seviyorum.**
boo shahr-kə-YƏ chohk seh-vih-yoh-ROOM

Come on, let's dance! **Hadi dans edelim!**
hah-DİH dahns eh-deh-LİHM!

Would you like to dance with me? **Dans etmek ister misin?**
dahns eht-MEHK ihs-TEHR mih-sihn?

I can't dance well. **İyi dans edemem.**
ih-YİH dahns eh-deh-MEHM

Come on, for my sake?	**Hadi ama, hatrım için?** *hah-DİH ah-MAH, haht-RƏM ih-CHİHN?*
I don't want to dance now, maybe a little later.	**Şimdi dans etmek istemiyorum, belki biraz sonra.** *shihm-DİH dahns eht-MEHK ihs-teh-mih-yoh-ROOM, behl-KİH bih-RAHZ sohn-RAH*
You dance very well.	**Çok iyi dans ediyorsun.** *chohk ih-YİH dahns eh-dih-yohr-SOON*
I want to get drunk!	**Sarhoş olmak istiyorum!** *sahr-HOHSH ohl-MAHK ihs-tih-yoh-ROOM!*

What are you drinking?	**Ne içiyorsun?** *neh ih-chih-yohr-SOON?*
Are you drunk?	**İçkili misin?** *ihch-kih-LİH mih-sihn?*
I'm drunk.	**Kafam iyi.** *kah-FAHM ih-YİH*

You shouldn't drink any more tonight.	**Bu gecelik içmesen artık.** *boo geh-jeh-LİHK ihch-meh-SEHN ahr-TƏK*
Are you okay?	**İyi misin?** *ih-YİH mih-sihn?*
I feel nauseous.	**Midem bulanıyor.** *mih-DEHM boo-lah-nə-YOHR*
I feel dizzy.	**Başım dönüyor.** *bah-SHƏM dö-nü-YOHR*
I'm leaving.	**Ben gidiyorum.** *behn gih-dih-yoh-ROOM*
Have fun.	**İyi eğlenceler.** *ih-YİH ehgh-lehn-jeh-LEHR*
Don't go yet!	**Henüz gitme!** *heh-NÜZ giht-MEH!*
Why are you leaving so early?	**Niye bu kadar erken gidiyorsun?** *nih-YEH boo kah-DAHR ehr-KEHN gih-dih-yohr-SOON?*
I'm very tired.	**Çok yorgunum.** *chohk yohr-goo-NOOM*
I have a headache.	**Başım ağrıyor.** *bah-SHƏM ahgh-rə-YOHR*

I can take you home if you want.	**Seni evine bırakabilirim istersen.** *seh-NİH eh-vih-NEH bə-rah-kah-bih-lih-RİHM ihs-tehr-SEHN*
Come on, let me drop you off at home.	**Hadi gel seni evine bırakayım.** *ha-DİH gehl seh-NİH eh-vih-NEH bə-rah-kah-YƏM*
Okay, let's go.	**Tamam, hadi gidelim.** *tah-MAHM, hah-DİH gih-deh-LİHM*
Can I have your number?	**Numaranı alabilir miyim?** *noo-mah-rah-NƏ ah-lah-bih-LİHR mih-yihm?*
My number is….	**Numaram** … *noo-mah-RAHM …*
Would you like a cup of coffee?	**Bir fincan kahve ister misin?** *bihr fihn-JAHN kahh-VEH ihs-TEHR mih-sihn?*
Would you like to come in?	**İçeriye gelmek ister misin?** *ih-cheh-rih-YEH gehl-MEHK ihs-TEHR mih-sihn?*

On the Phone 11

telephone	**telefon** *teh-leh-FOHN*
cell phone	**cep telefonu** *jehp teh-leh-foh-NOO*
Hello	**Alo / Efendim** *ah-LOH / eh-fehn-DİHM*

You can use either one. Keep in mind, though, that they are used only on the phone, not as in-person greetings.

May I speak to Can, please?	**Canla görüşebilir miyim?** *jahn-LAH gö-rü-sheh-bih-LİHR mih-yihm?*
Is Can there?	**Can orada mı?** *jahn oh-rah-DAH mə?*
Is Can at home?	**Can evde mi acaba?** *jahn ehv-DEH mih ah-jah-BAH?*
Who's calling?	**Kim arıyor?** *kihm ah-rə-YOHR?*
Who may I say is calling?	**Kim arıyor diyeyim?** *kihm ah-rə-YOHR dih-yeh-YİHM?*

Yes he's / she's here, one minute, please.	**Evet burada, bir dakika, lütfen.** *eh-VEHT boo-rah-DAH, bihr dah-kih-KAH lüt-FEHN*
Hold on.	**Bir saniye / Bir dakika.** *bihr sah-nih-YEH / bihr dah-kih-DAH*

Bir saniye means "one second," **bir dakika** means "one minute." Both can be used to mean "hold on" or "just a moment."

Could you wait a minute?	**Bir dakika bekler misin?** *bihr dah-kih-KAH behk-LEHR mih-sihn?*

This is a rhetorical question and the speaker actually means "hold on."

Can, it's for you!	**Can, telefonun var!** *jahn, teh-leh-foh-NOON vahr!*
I'm sorry to have kept you waiting.	**Beklettiğim için özür dilerim.** *behk-leht-tih-GHİHM ih-CHİHN ö-ZÜR dih-leh-RİHM*
I'm busy at the moment.	**Şu an meşgulüm.** *shoo ahn mehsh-goo-LÜM*
He / she is busy at the moment.	**Kendisi şu an meşgul.** *kehn-dih-SİH shoo ahn mehsh-GOOL*

Kendisi is a unisex word. You can use it for referring to either a female or a male.

Can isn't here right now.	**Can şu an burada değil.** *jahn shoo ahn boo-rah-DAH deh-GHİHL*

Can you call back later?	**Biraz sonra tekrar arar mısın?** *bih-RAHZ sohn-RAH tehk-RAHR ah-RAHR mə-sən?*
Do you have a message?	**Mesajınız var mı?** *meh-sah-zhə-nəz vahr mə?*
Would you like to leave a message?	**Mesaj bırakmak ister misiniz?** *meh-SAHZH bə-rahk-MAHK ihs-TEHR mih-sih-nihz?*
Can I leavc a message?	**Mesaj bırakabilir miyim?** *meh-SAHZH bə-rah-kah-bih-LİHR mih-yihm?*
Please tell him / her to call me back.	**Lütfen beni aramasını söyleyin.** *lüt-FEHN beh-NİH ah-rah-mah-sə-NƏ söy-leh-YİHN*
Please tell him / her that I called.	**Lütfen kendisine benim aradığımı söyleyin.** *lüt-FEHN kehn-dih-sih-NEH beh-NİHM ah-rah-də-ghə-MƏ söy-leh-YİHN*

Kendisine is a unisex word that can mean either "to him" or "to her."

Does he / she have your number?	**Numaranız var mı kendisinde?** *noo-mah-rah-NƏZ vahr mə kehn-dih-sihn-DEH?*
Would you like to leave your number?	**Numaranızı bırakmak ister misiniz?** *noo-mah-rah-nə-ZƏ bə-rahk-MAHK ihs-TEHR mih-sih-nihz?*

He / she has my number. — **Numaram var kendisinde.**
noo-mah-RAHM vahr kehn-dih-sihn-DEH

My number is… — **Numaram…**
noo-mah-RAHM…

Call me as soon as possible! — **Beni en kısa zamanda ara!**
beh-NİH ehn kə-SAH zah-mahn-DAH ah-RAH!

Call me when you get this message. — **Bu mesajı alınca beni ara.**
boo meh-sah-ZHƏ ah-lən-JAH beh-NİH ah-RAH

Do you know when he'll / she'll be back? — **Ne zaman döneceğini biliyor musunuz?**
neh zah-MAHN dö-neh-jeh-ghih-NİH bih-lih-YOHR moo-soo-nooz?

I guess he'll / she'll be back in an hour. — **Bir saat içinde gelir herhalde.**
bihr sah-AHT ih-chihn-DEH geh-LİHR hehr-hahl-DEH

Okay, I'll call him / her back later.	**Tamam, sonra ararım kendisini.** *tah-MAHM, sohn-RAH ah-rah-RƏM kehn-dih-sih-NİH*
Unfortunately I don't know.	**Maalesef bilmiyorum.** *mah-ah-leh-SEHF bihl-mih-yoh-ROOM*
All right, have a good day.	**Oldu, iyi günler.** *ohl-DOO, ih-yih gün-LEHR*

Getting Serious 12

I want to know more about you.	**Seni daha yakından tanımak istiyorum.** *seh-NİH dah-HAH yah-kənh-DAHN tah-nə-MAHK ihs-tih-yoh-ROOM*
Is it possible to get to know you more?	**Seni daha yakından tanımam mümkün mü?** *seh-NİH dah-HAH yah-kən-DAHN tah-nə-MAHM müm-KÜN mü?*
Shall we get together again?	**Tekrar buluşur muyuz?** *tehk-RAHR boo-loo-SHOOR moo-yooz?*
When can I see you again?	**Seni tekrar ne zaman göreceğim?** *seh-NİH tehk-RAHR neh zah-MAHN gö-reh-jeh-GHİHM?*
May I call you?	**Seni arayabilir miyim?** *seh-NİH ah-rah-yah-bih-LİHR mih-yihm?*
May I have your phone number?	**Numaranı alabilir miyim?** *noo-mah-rah-NƏ ah-lah-bih-LİHR mih-yihm?*

Take this, it's my phone number.	**Al, bu benim numaram.** *ahl, boo beh-NİHM noo-mah-RAHM*
My home number is...	**Ev telefon numaram...** *ehv teh-leh-FOHN noo-mah-RAHM...*
My cell phone number is...	**Cep telefon numaram...** *jehp teh-leh-FOHN noo-mah-RAHM...*
Are you going to call me?	**Beni arayacak mısın?** *beh-NİH ah-rah-yah-JAHK mə-sən?*
Call me.	**Ara beni.** *ah-RAH beh-NİH*
I've been thinking about you.	**Hep seni düşünüyorum.** *hehp seh-NİH dü-shü-nü-yoh-ROOM*
I want to see you.	**Seni görmek istiyorum.** *seh-NİH gör-MEHK ihs-tih-yoh-ROOM*
You're always on my mind.	**Hep aklımdasın.** *hehp ahk-ləm-dah-SƏN*
Can we meet now?	**Şimdi görüşebilir miyiz?** *shihm-DİH gö-rü-sheh-bih-LİHR mih-yihz?*
I can't go out now.	**Şimdi dışarıya çıkamam.** *shihm-DİH də-shah-rə-YAH chə-kah-MAHM*

I wrote you a letter.	**Sana bir mektup yazdım.** *sah-NAH bihr mehk-TOOP yahz-DƏM*
I'll write you a letter.	**Sana bir mektup yazacağım.** *sah-NAH bihr mehk-TOOP yah-zah-jah-GHƏM*
I wrote a poem for you.	**Senin için bir şiir yazdım.** *seh-NİHN ih-CHİHN bihr shih-İHR yahz-DƏM*
Don't cry.	**Ağlama.** *ahgh-lah-MAH*
Come on, wipe your tears.	**Hadi gözyaşlarını sil.** *hah-DİH göz-yahsh-lah-rə-NƏ sihl*
I can't stand being without you.	**Sensizliğe dayanamıyorum.** *sehn-sihz-lih-GHEH dah-yah-nah-mə-yoh-ROOM*
I can't be without you.	**Sensiz olamam.** *sehn-SİHZ oh-lah-MAHM*
Being without you is very difficult.	**Sensizlik çok zor.** *sehn-sihz-LİHK chohk zohr*
Will you be my girlfriend?	**Kız arkadaşım olur musun?** *kəz ahr-kah-dah-SHƏM oh-LOOR moo-soon?*

It's customary in Turkey for a man to ask a woman to be his girlfriend, not the other way around.

Lovers' Language 13

Do you have a girlfriend?	**Kız arkadaşın var mı?** *kəz ahr-kah-dah-SHƏN vahr mə?*
Do you have a boyfriend?	**Erkek arkadaşın var mı?** *ehr-KEHK ahr-kah-dah-SHƏN vahr mə?*
Are you dating anyone?	**Çıktığın biri var mı?** *chək-tə-GHƏN bih-RİH vahr mə?*
Are you married?	**Evli misin?** *ehv-LİH mih-sihn?*
I am married.	**Evliyim.** *ehv-lih-YİHM*
You're very pretty.	**Çok güzelsin.** *chohk gü-zehl-SİHN*
I adore you.	**Sana hayranım.** *sah-NAH hahy-rah-NƏM*
I like you (a lot).	**Senden (çok) hoşlanıyorum.** *sehn-DEHN (chohk) hohsh-lah-nə-yoh-ROOM*

I miss you (a lot).	**Seni (çok) özledim.** *seh-NİH (chohk) öz-leh-DİHM*
Did you miss me?	**Beni özledin mi?** *beh-NİH öz-leh-DİHN mih?*
Do you love me?	**Beni seviyor musun?** *beh-NİH seh-vih-YOHR moo-soon?*
I love you.	**Seni seviyorum.** *seh-NİH seh-vih-yoh-ROOM*
I am in love with you.	**Sana sırılsıklam aşığım.** *sah-NAH sə-rəl-sək-LAHM ah-shə-GHƏM*
I love you with all my heart.	**Seni tüm kalbimle seviyorum.** *seh-NİH tüm kahl-bihm-LEH seh-vih-yoh-ROOM*
I love Can.	**Canı seviyorum.** *jah-NƏ seh-vih-yoh-ROOM*
He / She loves me.	**O beni seviyor.** *oh beh-NİH seh-vih-YOHR*

The pronoun for "he" and "she" is the same: **o**.

You're handsome.	**Çok yakışıklısın.** *chohk yah-kə-shək-lə-SƏN*
You're very sexy.	**Çok seksisin.** *chohk sehk-sih-SİHN*

Are you jealous of me?
Kıskanıyor musun beni?
kəs-kah-nə-YOHR moo-soon beh-NİH?

I'm jealous of you.
Seni kıskanıyorum.
seh-NİH kəs-kah-nə-yoh-ROOM

You make me jealous.
Beni kıskandırıyorsun.
beh-NİH kəs-kahn-də-rə-yohr-SOON

There is no reason for you to be jealous of me.
Beni kıskanmanı gerektiren bir neden yok.
beh-NİH kəs-kahn-mah-NƏ geh-rehk-tih-REHN bihr neh-DEHN yohk

I need you.
Sana ihtiyacım var.
sah-NAH ihh-tih-yah-JƏM vahr

You're always on my mind.
Hep aklımdasın.
hehp ahk-ləm-dah-SƏN

You have beautiful eyes.
Çok güzel gözlerin var.
chohk gü-ZEHL göz-leh-RİHN vahr

You are a hot chick.
Fıstık gibisin.
fəs-TƏK gih-bih-SİHN

Fıstık means "peanut" so this expression literally means "you are like a peanut." It's used by men for beautiful women, meant as a compliment.

I adore your smile.
Gülüşüne hayranım.
gü-lü-shü-NEH hahy-rah-NƏM

I love your smile.	**Gülüşünü çok seviyorum.** *gü-lü-shü-NÜ chohk seh-vih-yoh-ROOM*
May I kiss you?	**Seni öpebilir miyim?** *seh-NİH ö-peh-bih-LİHR mih-yihm?*

Kiss me.	**Öp beni.** *öp beh-NİH*
I want to kiss you.	**Seni öpmek istiyorum.** *seh-NİH öp-MEHK ihs-tih-yoh-ROOM*
Look into my eyes.	**Gözlerime bak.** *göz-leh-rih-MEH bahk*
Look at me.	**Bana bak.** *bah-NAH bahk*
Come closer to me.	**Yaklaş bana.** *yahk-LAHSH bah-NAH*
Hug me.	**Kucakla beni.** *koo-jahk-LAH beh-NİH*

I desire you.	**Seni arzuluyorum.** *seh-NİH ahr-zoo-loo-yoh-ROOM*
Touch me.	**Dokun bana.** *doh-KOON bah-NAH*
Harder.	**Daha kuvvetli.** *dah-HAH koov-veht-LİH*
Softer.	**Daha yumuşak.** *dah-HAH yoo-moo-SHAHK*
Faster.	**Daha hızlı.** *dah-HAH həz-LƏ*
Slower.	**Daha yavaş.** *dah-HAH yah-VAHSH*
Deeper.	**Daha derin.** *dah-HAH deh-RİHN*
I am coming.	**Boşalıyorum / Geliyorum.** *boh-shah-lə-yoh-ROOM / geh-lih-yoh-ROOM*
Did you come?	**Boşaldın mı / geldin mi?** *boh-shahl-DƏN mə / gehl-DİHN mih?*
That was amazing.	**Harikaydı.** *hah-rih-kahy-DƏ*
One more time.	**Bir kez daha.** *bihr kehz dah-HAH*

Do you want to stay with me tonight?	**Bu gece benimle kalmak ister misin?** *boo geh-JEH beh-nihm-LEH kahl-MAHK ihs-TEHR mih-sihn?*
I want to stay with you tonight.	**Bu gece seninle kalmak istiyorum.** *boo geh-JEH seh-nihn-LEH kahl-MAHK ihs-tih-yoh-ROOM*
I feel very close to you.	**Kendimi sana çok yakın hissediyorum.** *kehn-dih-MİH sah-NAH chohk yah-KƏN hihs-seh-dih-yoh-ROOM*
Don't go!	**Gitme!** *giht-MEH!*
You are the light of my life.	**Hayatımın ışığısın.** *hah-yah-tə-MƏN ə-shə-ghə-SƏN*
Do you want to have sex with me?	**Benimle seks yapmak ister misin?** *beh-nihm-LEH sehks yahp-MAHK ihs-TEHR mih-sihn?*
Do you want me?	**Beni istiyor musun?** *beh-NİH ihs-tih-YOHR moo-soon?*
I want you.	**Seni istiyorum.** *seh-NİH ihs-tih-yoh-ROOM*

I don't have sex with just anyone I meet.
Önüme çıkan herkesle yatmam.
ö-nü-MEH chə-KAHN hehr-kehs-LEH yaht-MAHM

I want to make love to you.
Seninle sevişmek istiyorum.
seh-nihn-LEH seh-vihsh-MEHK ihs-tih-yoh-ROOM

Close your eyes.
Gözlerini kappa.
göz-leh-rih-NİH kah-PAH

I'm still a virgin.
Ben hala bakireyim.
behn hah-LAH bah-kih-reh-YİHM

I'm pregnant.
Hamileyim.
hah-mih-leh-YİHM

I don't want to get pregnant.
Hamile kalmak istemiyorum.
hah-mih-LEH kahl-MAHK ihs-teh-mih-yoh-ROOM

I'm afraid of getting pregnant.
Hamile kalmaktan korkuyorum.
hah-mih-LEH kahl-mahk-TAHN kohr-koo-yoh-ROOM

You must use a condom.	**Prezervatif kullanmalısın.** *preh-zehr-vah-TİHF kool-lahn-mah-lə-SƏN*
I'll use a condom.	**Prezervatif kullanacağım.** *preh-zehr-vah-TİHF kool-lah-nah-jah-GHƏM*
Are you on the Pill?	**Doğum kontrol hapı kullanıyor musun?** *doh-GHOOM kohnt-ROHL hah-PƏ kool-lah-nə-YOHR moo-soon?*
You are my one and only.	**Sen benim tekimsin.** *sehn beh-NİHM teh-kihm-SİHN*
You are the love of my life.	**Sen hayatımın aşkısın.** *sehn hah-yah-tə-MƏN ahsh-kə-SƏN*
You are my everything.	**Sen benim her şeyimsin.** *sehn beh-NİHM hehr sheh-yihm-SİHN*
You are my heaven.	**Sen benim cennetimsin.** *sehn beh-NİHM jehn-neh-tihm-SİHN*
You are my soul mate.	**Sen benim ruhumun eşisin.** *sehn beh-NİHM roo-hoo-MOON eh-shih-SİHN*
I fell in love with you at first sight.	**Sana ilk görüşte aşık oldum.** *sah-NAH ihlk gö-rüsh-TEH ah-SHƏK ohl-DOOM*

My life	**Hayatım** *hah-yah-TƏM*
My soul	**Canım** *jah-NƏM*
My love	**Aşkım** *ahsh-KƏM*
My only one	**Bir tanem** *bihr tah-NEHM*
My baby	**Bebeğim** *beh-beh-GHİHM*
My darling	**Sevgilim** *sehv-gih-LİHM*
My sweetie	**Tatlım** *taht-LƏM*

Notice that in Turkish, you don't say terms of endearments alone but add "my" at the beginning of it.

Will you marry me?	**Benimle evlenir misin?** *beh-nihm-LEH ehv-leh-NİHR mih-sihn?*

Trouble in Paradise 14

Are you still mad at me?	**Hala bana kızgın mısın?** *hah-LAH bah-NAH kəz-GƏN mə-sən?*
You're hurting my feelings.	**Duygularımı incitiyorsun.** *dooy-goo-lah-rə-MƏ ihn-jih-tih-yohr-SOON*
You're breaking my heart.	**Kalbimi kırıyorsun.** *kahl-bih-MİH kə-rə-yohr-SOON*

I didn't mean to hurt your feelings.	**Duygularını incitmek istemezdim.** *dooy-goo-lah-rə-NƏ ihn-ciht-MEHK ihs-teh-mehz-DİHM*
I didn't mean to make you sad.	**Seni üzmek istemezdim.** *seh-NİH üz-MEHK ihs-teh-mehz-DİHM*

Are you lying to me? **Bana yalan mı söylüyorsun?**
bah-NAH yah-LAHN mə söy-lü-yohr-SOON?

You are lying to me! **Bana yalan söylüyorsun!**
bah-NAH yah-LAHN söy-lü-yohr-SOON!

You lied to me! **Bana yalan söyledin!**
bah-NAH yah-LAHN söy-leh-DİHN!

Why did you lie to me? **Niye bana yalan söyledin?**
nih-YEH bah-NAH yah-LAHN söy-leh-DİHN?

I had trusted you. **Sana güvenmiştim.**
sah-NAH gü-vehn-mihsh-TİHM

I made a mistake trusting you! **Sana güvenmekle hata yaptım!**
sah-NAH gü-vehn-mehk-LEH hah-TAH yahp-TƏM!

I called you many times, why didn't you answer? **Seni defalarca aradım, niye cevap vermedin?**
seh-NİH deh-fah-lahr-JAH ah-rah-DƏM, nih-YEH jeh-VAHP vehr-meh-DİHN?

You don't understand me! **Beni anlamıyorsun!**
beh-NİH ahn-lah-mə-yohr-SOON!

I'm not happy with you anymore. **Seninle mutlu değilim artık.**
seh-nihn-LEH moot-LOO deh-ghih-LİHM ahr-TƏK

I need time to think.	**Düşünmek için zamana ihtiyacım var.** *dü-shün-MEHK ih-CHİHN zah-mah-NAH ihh-tih-yah-JƏM vahr*
I don't love you anymore!	**Seni sevmiyorum artık!** *seh-NİH sehv-mih-yoh-ROOM ahr-TƏK!*
Is there another woman in your life?	**Hayatında başka bir kadın mı var?** *hah-yah-tən-DAH bahsh-KAH bihr kah-DƏN mə vahr?*
Is there another man in your life?	**Hayatında başka bir erkek mi var?** *hah-yah-tən-DAH bahsh-KAH bihr ehr-KEHK mih vahr?*
I know you're cheating on me.	**Beni aldattığını biliyorum.** *beh-NİH ahl-daht-tə-ghə-NƏ bih-lih-yoh-ROOM*
Don't play with my emotions!	**Duygularımla oynama!** *dooy-goo-lah-rəm-LAH ohy-nah-MAH!*
You are stone hearted!	**Sen bir taş kalplisin!** *sehn bihr tahsh kahlp-lih-SİHN!*
How could you do this to me!	**Bunu bana nasıl yaparsın!** *boo-NOO bah-NAH nah-SƏL yah-pahr-SƏN!*

I didn't expect this from you! — **Bunu senden beklemezdim!** *boo-NOO sehn-DEHN behk-leh-mehz-DİHM!*

For me to forgive you is impossible! — **Seni affetmem imkansız!** *seh-NİH ahf-feht-MEHM ihm-kahn-SƏZ!*

It's impossible for me to trust you again. — **Sana tekrar güvenebilmem imkansız.** *sah-NAH tehk-RAHR gü-veh-neh-bihl-MEHM ihm-kahn-SƏZ*

I don't trust you. — **Sana güvenmiyorum.** *sah-NAH gü-vehn-mih-yoh-ROOM*

I don't believe you. — **Sana inanmıyorum.** *sah-NAH ih-nahn-mə-yoh-ROOM*

It's best not to see each other anymore. — **Artık görüşmesek iyi olur.** *ahr-TƏK gö-rüsh-meh-SEHK ih-YİH oh-LOOR*

Let's not see each other anymore. — **Artık görüşmeyelim.** *ahr-TƏK gö-rüsh-meh-yeh-lihm*

We have to break up. — **Ayrılmalıyız.** *ahy-rəl-mah-lə-YƏZ*

I love someone else. — **Başka birini seviyorum.** *bahsh-KAH bih-rih-NİH seh-vih-yoh-ROOM*

I like you but I don't love you.	**Senden hoşlanıyorum ama seni sevmiyorum.** *sehn-DEHN hohsh-lah-nə-yoh-ROOM ah-MAH seh-NİH sehv-mih-yoh-ROOM*
I hate you!	**Senden nefret ediyorum!** *sehn-DEHN nehf-REHT eh-dih-yoh-ROOM!*
Please, don't hate me.	**Nolur benden nefret etme.** *noh-LOOR behn-DEHN nehf-REHT eht-MEH*

Nolur is like "pretty please." In the above sentence, you could also use **lütfen** (please).

I know you hate me.	**Benden nefret ettiğini biliyorum.** *behn-DEHN nehf-REHT eht-tih-ghih-NİH bih-lih-yoh-ROOM*
I don't care about you!	**Umrumda değilsin!** *oom-room-DAH deh-ghihl-SİHN!*
Our relationship is over.	**İlişkimiz bitti.** *ih-lihsh-kih-MİHZ biht-TİH*
I won't call you anymore.	**Seni bir daha aramayacağım.** *seh-NİH bihr dah-HAH ah-rah-mah-yah-jah-GHƏM*
Don't call me anymore!	**Beni bir daha arama!** *beh-NİH bihr dah-HAH ah-rah-MAH!*

Don't bother me anymore!
Beni rahatsız etme artık!
beh-NİH rah-haht-SƏZ eht-MEH ahr-TƏK!

Leave me alone!
Beni yalnız bırak!
beh-NİH yahl-NƏZ bə-RAHK!

Get out of my life!
Defol hayatımdan!
deh-FOHL hah-yah-təm-DAHN!

Can't we start over?
Yeniden başlayamaz mıyız?
yeh-nih-DEHN bahsh-lah-yah-MAHZ mə-yəz?

Please, let's end it amicably.
Lütfen dostça bitirelim.
lüt-FEHN dohst-CHAH bih-tih-reh-LİHM

I will miss you a lot.
Seni çok özleyeceğim.
seh-NİH chohk öz-leh-yeh-jeh-GHİHM

I will never forget you.
Seni hiç unutmayacağım.
seh-NİH hihch oo-noot-mah-yah-jah-GHƏM

Can we still be friends?
Arkadaş kalabilir miyiz?
ahr-kah-DAHSH kah-lah-bih-LİHR mih-yihz?

We can be friends, if you want.
Arkadaş kalabiliriz, istersen.
ahr-kah-DAHSH kah-lah-bih-lih-RİHZ, ihs-tehr-SEHN

Unfortunately, that's not a good idea. **Maalesef, bu iyi bir fikir değil.**
mah-ah-leh-SEHF, boo ih-YİH bihr fih-KİHR deh-GHİHL

I hope you'll be happy with her / him. **Onunla mutlu olmanı diliyorum.**
oh-noon-LAH moot-LOO ohl-mah-Nə dih-lih-yoh-ROOM

This is a unisex sentence; **onunla** can mean either "with him" or "with her."

I'll always love you. **Seni her zaman seveceğim.**
seh-NİH hehr zah-MAHN seh-veh-jeh-GHİHM

Goodbye. **Elveda.**
ehl-veh-DAH

This is used only when you intend to say goodbye for good.

Expressions & Proverbs

"The genius, wit and spirit of a nation are discovered in its proverbs."
—*Francis Bacon*

"Arabic is a language, Persian is a sweetmeat; Turkish is an art."
—*Persian proverb*

Turkey has a rich cultural heritage and the Turkish language reflects this richness through colorful expressions and idioms, drawing on folk wisdom and shared experience. Turkish has an expression or idiom for almost every occasion.

Since sometimes the literal translation from one language to another might not render what was meant, I've included explanations to convey the intended meanings. Along with the expressions' wisdom, you'll notice their abundance of good intention, sense of humor and rhyme. These phrases will help you not only to sound like a natural in your conversations with Turkish people, but also to express your wishes to your new Turkish friends more precisely!

Hoş geldin.
(hohsh gehl-dihn)
Welcome.
Expression used by a host.

Hoş bulduk.
(hohsh bool-dook)
Glad to be here.
Expression used by the arriving visitor.

Eline sağlık.
(eh-lih-neh sahgh-lək)
Bless your hands.
Expression used to compliment the person who cooked a meal.

Afiyet olsun.
(ah-fih-yeht ohl-soon)
Enjoy your meal.
Literally, "May what you eat bring you well-being." It's similar to the saying "bon appetit," and it can be used either at the beginning of a meal or at the end of it. It's also used as a response by the host when someone says "**eline saglık**."

Ziyade olsun.
(zih-yah-deh ohl-soon)
May you always enjoy abundance.
This expression is used at the end of a meal, although not as commonly as "**ellerine sağlık**." It's often used when you finish a glass of tea and you would like to indicate that you want no more.

Maşallah
(mah-shahl-lahh)
Conveying "May God protect from the evil eye or misfortune," you would use this when giving someone a compliment, especially about a child. Ex.: "Your child is so smart, **Maşallah**."

İnşallah
(ihn-shahl-lahh)
God willing
Used when talking about future events. Ex.: "**İnşallah**, I'll pass my math exam tomorrow."

Kolay gelsin
(koh-lahy gehl-sihn)
May it be easy
An expression used when you see someone working or busy with something, to offer your wish that the person's task will go smoothly.

Geçmiş olsun
(gehch-mihsh ohl-soon)
Get well soon

Başın sağ olsun
(bah-shən sahgh ohl-soon)
My condolences
The response to this is **Dostlar sağolsun** which literally means "May friends be well." It's used to convey "thank you" in this context.

İyi şanslar
(ih-yih shahns-lahr)
Good luck

Şükürler olsun
(shü-kür-lehr ohl-soon)
Thank God

Öyle istiyorsan öyle olsun
(öy-leh ihs-tih-yohr-sahn öy-leh ohl-soon)
If you wish it that way, let it be. / Do whatever you want!
You'd use this when you give advice to someone or when you don't agree with someone about something, yet he/she insists on doing it his/her way. You'd say this to throw in the towel, so to speak.

Doğum günün kutlu olsun
(doh-ghoom gü-nün koot-loo ohl-soon)
Happy birthday

Mutlu yıllar
(moot-loo yəl-lahr)
Happy years
This is what you would say to your partner when celebrating your wedding anniversary. It expresses your wish that you'll spend many years to come together. You can also use this expression for birthdays, new year's celebrations, or similar occasions. You are conveying that you wish to spend many more of that occasion with the person you're saying it to.

Senin paran burada geçmez
(seh-nihn pah-rahn boo-rah-dah gehch-mehz)
Your money is of no value here.
Used by someone who insists on picking up the tab. In Turkish culture, when people go out to a restaurant, they do not like to divide the bill. Usually one person will pay the whole tab and another can pay for the next time. In the same way, in a bar or a nightclub, one buys a round of drinks for everyone and another buys the next round as opposed to everyone buying his/her own drink.

Tebrik ederim
(tehb-rihk eh-deh-rihm)
Congratulations

Aferin sana!
(ah-feh-rihn sah-nah)
Well done!

Allah analı babalı büyütsün
(ahl-lahh ah-nah-lə bah-bah-lə bü-yüt-sün)
May God bring up your child with both a father and a mother
Well wishing expression used for new parents.

Çok yaşa
(chohk yah-shah)
Bless you
Literally, it means "live long." This is what is said in Turkey when someone sneezes.

Sen de gör
(sehn deh gör)
You'd say this as a response, when you sneeze and someone says "bless you." In this context, it means "you too."

Güle güle kullan / Hayırlı olsun
(gü-leh gü-leh kool-lahn / hah-yər-lə ohl-soon)
May you use it smiling / may it be blessed
Expression you would use when someone buys or receives something new and you want to convey your well-wishing sentiments.

Dost için çiğ tavuk bile yenir
(dohst ih-chihn chihgh tah-vook bih-leh yeh-nihr)
For a good friend, even a raw chicken is eaten.
Emphasizes the value of friendship and that you should always stand by your friend.

Gözün aydın
(gö-zün ahy-dən)
You would use this to express that you share the speaker's joy, when he shares with you that something he has been longing for came true.

Selam söyle
(seh-lahm söy-leh)
Say hello from me

Yolun açık olsun
(yoh-loon ah-chək ohl-soon)
Expression used for someone who is about to travel, wishing him a safe journey. Literal meaning: "may your road be open."

Hayırlı işler
(hah-yər-lə ihsh-lehr)
Expression said to someone who is on his or her way to work, or to the shopkeeper when you are leaving a store. It means "may you have a good working day."

Isıracak köpek havlamaz.
(ə-sə-rah-jahk kö-pehk hahv-lah-mahz)
Lit. The dog that will bite doesn't bark.
Fig. Don't threaten that you'll do something, just do it!

Sinek küçüktür, ama mide bulandırır.
(sih-nehk kü-chük-tür ah-mah mih-deh boo-lahn-də-rər)
Lit. The fly is small, but it is big enough to make one sick.
Fig. An event that seems insignificant to others could still bother a person.

Gülünü seven dikenine katlanır.
(gü-lü-nü seh-vehn dih-keh-nih-neh kaht-lah-nər)
Lit. If you love roses, you endure their thorns.

Su uyur düşman uyumaz
(soo oo-yoor, düsh-mahn oo-yoo-mahz)
Lit. Water sleeps, enemy doesn't.
Fig. Be watchful of your enemies.

Ayıpsız dost arayan dostsuz kalır
(ah-yəp-səz dohst ah-rah-yahn dohst-sooz kah-lər)
Lit. He who looks for a friend without fault will be without a friend.

Demir nemden, insan gamdan çürür.
(deh-mihr nehm-dehn, ihn-sahn gahm-dahn chü-rür)
Lit. Iron deteriorates with dampness, human deteriorates with worry.

Tatsız aşa tuz neylesin, akılsız başa söz neylesin
(taht-səz ah-shah tooz nehy-leh-sihn, ah-kəl-səz bah-shah söz nehy-leh-sihn)
Lit. Salt doesn't do any good to a tasteless meal, advice doesn't do any good to a head with no mind.

Cennet anaların ayağı altındadır.
(jehn-neht ah-nah-lah-rən ah-yah-ghə ahl-tən-dah-dər)
Lit. Paradise lies under the feet of mothers.
This saying expresses the value placed on mothers in Turkish culture.

Körler çarşısında ayna satma, sağırlar çarşısında gazel atma
(kör-lehr chahr-shə-sən-dah ahy-nah saht-mah, sah-ghər-lahr chahr-shə-sən-dah gah-zehl aht-mah)
Lit. Don't sell mirrors among blind people, don't sing a song among deaf people.
Fig. Everything has a right place and a right time.

Köpeğin duası kabul olsaydı, gökden kemik yağardı.
(kö-peh-ghihn doo-ah-sə kah-bool ohl-sahy-də, gök-tehn keh-mihk yah-ghahr-də)
Lit. If a prayer of a dog were answered, bones would rain from the sky.
This comeback is used as a response to someone who's wished bad fortune on you.

Körle yatan şaşı kalkar.
(kör-leh yah-tahn shah-shə kahl-kahr)
Lit. He who sleeps with a blind man will wake up cross-eyed.

İmam osurursa cemaat sıçar.
(ih-mahm oh-soo-roor-sah, jeh-mah-aht sə-chahr)
Lit. If the imam farts, his followers shit.
Fig. The leader serves as a model for the people.
In Islam, the imam is the religious leader of a mosque.

Bıçak yarası geçer, dil yarası geçmez
(bə-chahk yah-rah-sə geh-chehr, dihl yah-rah-sə gehch-mehz)
Lit. A knife wound heals, a wound caused by words lingers.

Armut dibine düşer.
(ahr-moot dih-bih-neh dü-shehr)
Lit. A pear falls close to the root.
Fig. An apple doesn't fall far from the tree.

Bir kahvenin kırk yıl hatırı vardır.
(bihr kahh-veh-nihn kərk yəl hah-tə-rə vahr-dər)
A cup of coffee commits one to forty years of friendship.
Used to express the value of friendship.

Al elmaya taş atan çok olur.
(ahl ehl-mah-yah tahsh ah-tahn chohk oh-loor)
Lit. There are too many people who throw stones at a red apple.
Fig. Good will be envied.

Beterin beteri vardır.
(beh-teh-rihn beh-teh-rih vahr-dər)
Lit. Every bad has its worse.
Things can always become even worse and one should always be grateful about his or her current situation, no matter how bad it is.

Denize düşen yılana sarılır.
(deh-nih-zeh dü-shehn yə-lah-nah sah-rə-lər)
Lit. The one who falls into the sea, grabs even a snake.
Fig. You may have to make an unpleasant choice in a dire situation.

Nerede birlik, orada dirlik.
(neh-reh-deh bihr-lihk, oh-rah-dah dihr-lihk)
Lit. Where there's unity there's harmony.

Sütten dili yanan yoğurdu üfleye üfleye yer.
(süt-tehn dih-lih yah-nahn yoh-ghoor-doo üf-leh-yeh üf-leh-yeh yehr)
Lit. One who burnt his mouth while drinking hot milk eats yoghurt carefully.
Fig. Once bitten, twice shy

Emek olmadan yemek olmaz.
(eh-mehk ohl-mah-dahn yeh-mehk ohl-mahz)
Lit. Without effort, there is no food.
Fig. No pain, no gain.

Vakit nakittir.
(vah-kiht nah-kiht-tihr)
Lit. Time is money.

Güler yüzlü sirke satıcısı, ekşi yüzlü bal satıcısından fazla para kazanır
(gü-lehr yüz-lü sihr-keh sah-tə-jə-sə, ehk-shih yüz-lü bahl sah-tə-jə-sən-dahn fahz-lah pah-rah kah-zah-nər)
Lit. A vinegar seller with a smiling face makes more money than a honey seller with a sour face.

Kör ölünce badem gözlü, kel ölünce sırma saçlı olur.
(kör ö-lün-jeh bah-dehm göz-lü, kehl ö-lün-jeh sər-mah sach-lə oh-loor)
Lit. When a blind man dies, everyone remembers the beautiful eyes he had; when a bald man dies, everyone remembers the golden hair he had.
This idiom expresses the exaggerated praise for the past.